LICENSE TO FALL

*Lessons From Motorcycling On
Pursuing A Life Of Your Choice*

ANIL NAIR

STARDOM BOOKS

www.StardomBooks.com

STARDOM BOOKS
112 Bordeaux Ct.
Coppell, TX 75019, USA

Copyright © 2024 by Anil Nair

All rights reserved. No part of this book may be reproduced or used in any manner without written permission of the copyright owner except for the use of quotations in a book review.

FIRST EDITION MAY 2024

STARDOM BOOKS, LLC.
112 Bordeaux Ct. Coppell, TX 75019, USA

www.stardombooks.com

Stardom Books, United States
Stardom Alliance, India

The author and publishers have made all reasonable efforts to contact copyright holders for permission and apologize for any omissions or errors in the form of credits given. Corrections may be made to future editions.

LICENSE TO FALL
Lessons From Motorcycling On Pursuing A Life Of Your Choice

ANIL NAIR

p. 160
cm. 13.97x21.59

Category:
BUS107000 – Business & Economics: Personal Success
SEL027000 – Self-Help: Personal Growth: Success

ISBN: 978-1-957456-44-7

DEDICATION

This book is dedicated to my parents Radha and Sadasivan, for everything they have done for me unconditionally and for teaching me the biggest life lesson – 'life is relationships.'
I bow to you.

CONTENTS

	ACKNOWLEDGEMENTS	i
	FOREWORD	iii
1.	INTRODUCTION	1
2.	EMBRACING THE UNKNOWN	11
3.	BEING PREPARED	29
4.	CALCULATED RISKS AND TRUSTING YOUR INSTINCTS	47
5.	FOCUS ON THE JOURNEY AND NOT THE DESTINATION	61
6.	CONCENTRATE ON THE ROAD, NOT THE OBSTACLES	73
7.	AVOID SHORTCUTS	85
8.	KNOW YOUR LIMITS	97
9.	THE FALL IS NOT THE END	105
10.	BE KIND TO STRANGERS	121
11.	MAKE YOUR OWN RULES	131
12.	CONCLUSION	141
13.	ABOUT THE AUTHOR	147

ACKNOWLEDGEMENTS

My heartfelt gratitude to Arati, my wife—- for putting up with all my crazy ideas and idiosyncrasies and Avantika, the apple of my eye— nothing comes close to the joy of watching you grow up and become the beautiful soul that you are.

To Mini, my sister—- for inspiring me with your ability to walk through walls no matter how thick they were.

To Rajkumar, my friend in heaven—- for showing me what selflessness really is.

To Meera and Anjana— for believing in 'us' and being there.

To my soul buddies from Trivandrum—- each of you have shaped my character in ways you can't imagine.

To Imtiaz, Joy, Avijit, Rakesh, Nassif—- for being the 'Bhai log' in every sense of the word.

To PK, Anil, and Sandy— for giving me the privilege to be a part of the most exciting and ambitious company building stories in the history of Indian advertising. A special mention to Sandy for the name Goodwind.

To John and Amit—- for believing and making my dream – Goodwind Moto Tours, come alive.

To the scores of clients who became friends, mentors and most importantly sources of inspiration with their amazing wisdom. The generous hours you gave me are a treasure trove of learning which have found its place in many chapters. You know who you are.

To the millions of motorcyclists out there, exploring our beautiful planet and reaching far flung corners braving every obstacle— you are the true inspiration for this book.

To my divine, for not forgetting me every moment of every day even though I have forgotten you for days together. This is your blessing and nothing else.

Lastly, to the Stardom team—- Sthitodhi Das, Rekha Krishnaprasad and Raam Anand for helping me throughout this journey.

FOREWORD

I remember with greatest delight when I once fell while riding a motorbike in the Delhi cold. The surface of the road was very warm; it was desolate, and I was alone. The indicator of the fallen bike was at eye level, and I felt a sense of contentment. I remember telling myself in that moment before I got up and set everything right, "Let's rest a while… let's rest a while!"

That is one of many qualifiers for me to write this Foreword. Anil Nair is one of the smartest people I know. He has chosen me carefully to write this Foreword. He is well aware of my various falls- failing in the ninth standard and having to repeat it, failing the entrance of mass communication at Jamia University, failing to get into any goddamn advertising agency in Bombay - I tried in all, and I tried desperately. Anil was there to see me fail each time. And he also saw me get up and take with vengeance the only job offer I had, that of a production assistant at Zee TV. Within the year, I was directing my first show on television.

"It is not how you fall; it is how you pick yourself up" - Anil Nair.

Fear is as essential in life as a villain in a movie. To confront fear constructs personality, but when I think about what works for me in confronting fear, the things that come to mind are not prolific. Like in childhood, I feared crossing a dark alley to my aunt's house. I did not believe in ghosts, but I was scared of them, and I did not want to run across the alley quickly. I chose each time to walk across slowly and casually. Do you know why? Because the ghosts that did not exist would see that I was a cool guy.

It is silly, but I have overcome many fears to appear like the cool guy. You are probably a biker, and you know what I mean. You people go a distance to be a 'cool guy.'

So, you have in your hands those precious words that I have heard from Anil sitting on footpaths, at bus stops, at bars playing loud rock music, and in the tranquility of distant beaches – words that come to me like waves each time I fall.

Enjoy this book, now that you have it – it will never leave you. I hope that the LICENSE TO FALL makes your ride sexier. Peace.

Imtiaz Ali,
Storyteller & Filmmaker

INTRODUCTION

There are only two ways to go from this world— One is with memories and the other one is with dreams. You can either say, "Yes, I did it!" or you can say "I wish I had done that!" I have met many people who chose to live their lives with their dreams in the cold storage because they have a fear of failing while pursuing their dreams. I have also met some whose lives are full of stories and memories of the highs and lows that they experienced while on the journey called life. Here is a question to you: What are you going to pack in the little suitcase of yours when you set out on your journey to the other worlds? Dreams or memories? For me, the purpose of life is to create memories that act as a source of inspiration for someone to live their life purposefully.

I had twenty-seven wonderful years of a career in advertising and marketing. One fine morning I gave it all up, started a few ventures, and most importantly, converted my passion for motorcycling into a business. Advertising gave me everything I have in life. I was fortunate to be given the opportunity to build a top-10 advertising company from scratch along with my partners in India at a time when the industry was getting dominated by global giants. I sat on the global board of one of the most famous advertising agencies in the world and ended up creating some iconic campaigns and brands. But something kept tugging me from the inside once I reached a certain level of professional success. All through my life, I have thrived during uncertainty. The adrenaline of challenges or the unknown always drove me. When I think about how my life journey has shaped me, it was my comfort with the unknown that shaped my destiny.

I come from the sleepy state capital of Kerala called Thiruvananthapuram (Trivandrum then). None of my friends or acquaintances were looking at advertising as a career. Everyone was preparing to become a computer engineer as it was the dream career in the early 90s in India. I did not even know the critical factors to succeed in the advertising business nor did I know where to look for that information. My parents took a punt (against many opinions from well-wishers) and I packed my bags one day and came to Mumbai- the mecca of Indian advertising. I joined a prestigious college and learned less about marketing and advertising and a lot about surviving in a big city with hardly any money. I built my entire professional career here in a city I never knew before. I have moved from very well-known ad agencies to unknown ad agencies (start-up was not a term used much at that time). I liked the challenge of building something from scratch rather than being comfortable in an established set up. So, every time I got comfortable, I repeated the same pattern of jumping into the uncertain side of the world. I love the excitement of chasing the unknown right through my life.

This may be the reason why I love motorcycles. Right from a young age, I loved the thrill of two wheels and the feeling of the wind in my face. I love the uncertainty around a motorcycle where your chances of a fall are much higher than the safety and stability of a four- wheeler. As the first born in an Indian middle-class family my designated seat was on the petrol tank of my father's motorcycle where my mother held my younger sister in her arms as a pillion. We went for our weekend outings, friends, and family visits and for movies, playing the dangerous stunt of four on two wheels like almost the entire country. A four-wheeler came home much later in our lives when we could no longer pull off the 'great Indian road trick' because of two kids who were outgrowing their clothes every year. My father loved his motorcycle so much that the motorcycle had more mileage in its odometer than the car at home. I suspect my obsession with these machines on two wheels is a genetic defect that got passed on.

One of the first possessions that I acquired when I got my first job was a pre-owned (Parsi owned to be precise) Yezdi motorcycle. It was my dream to own one right from my college days. A year into riding that motorcycle I had a near-fatal accident that could have ended my riding phase of life forever. To everyone's surprise when I recovered from the accident, I got myself another motorcycle and continued riding as if nothing happened. I must confess that had my parents, especially my father, not helped with some money and their silent support, I would have ended my love affair with two wheels then. Never had he once told me to stop the madness with my motorcycling and opt for a safer form of transport. As life took its course, I finally had to move to the four wheels, but I always had this secret love for motorcycles in my heart.

After almost twenty years of giving up motorcycling, I returned to my former love. Though India is one of the largest two-wheeler markets in the world, 99% of all motorcycles sold are commuter vehicles with little or no excitement factor for the true motorheads. But by the turn of the millennium, we started seeing some world class motorcycle brands bringing in their best products to attract the growing leisure motorcycling enthusiasts in India. A test ride on a few and soon I realized what I had been missing all these years and above all how alive

I felt on top of these wonderful machines. From one motorcycle to two to three, my garage parking was getting full. Today, I am a proud co-founder of India's premier motorcycle touring company - Goodwind Moto Tours (GMT).

With charity at the core, I have brought together my passion for motorcycles and passion to make a difference to the lives of the underprivileged and created a wonderful organization with two of my dear friends and partners. We take motorcyclists on a guided tour across India, the Alps, Balkans, Greece, Italy, South Africa, Namibia, and Thailand. GMT now has a large fan following and some of them plan their holiday calendar based on our ride calendar.

Today, I must say that I am the master of my time. I enjoy every minute that I spend on my businesses. I wear multiple hats such as Executive Director of a very successful business consulting company (Equitor Value Advisory), Board of Director of a billion-dollar listed company (Kalyan Jewellers), board member of a few soon to be billion-dollar companies (Packfora, Ennovate Fashion ltd) and run a few of my businesses like GMT. I am able to work across all these ventures and add value to them simply because I have allowed life to flow and use my passion as my navigator.

So, why did I write this book?

I have fallen many times from my motorcycle and in life as well. Some of the falls have been quite significant and have altered my life totally. However, my reaction to each one of the falls allowed me to continue my course as I wanted. If I had feared the next fall, my life trajectory would have been different. I certainly learned about the factors that led to the fall so that I could improve myself and not repeat the same mistake. I also understand myself better after each setback. And I have avoided certain pitfalls but could not avoid another fall altogether. 'Falls are a way of life' is a lesson that I have learned early enough in life. I had to make adjustments and alterations, but I never abandoned the journey.

In December 2019, I hung up my corporate shoes for a series of new businesses, including Goodwind Moto Tours and my consulting business. I was inundated with calls from across my circle. Many of them congratulated me for my courage to take such a bold step in life. Through my conversations over many cups of coffee and glasses of wine, I figured that almost everyone was sitting with a wish-list of what they would love to do in life but couldn't because they feared that they wouldn't be able to afford a 'failure.' I became a bouncing board/guide to help them see if they were too late to set out in the direction they always wanted. They wanted a playbook, or they wanted to know if they could copy my playbook.

COVID and the subsequent lockdowns gave me time, so I started to delve a little deeper into this topic. I was able to have many such conversations over Zoom calls with an eclectic mix of people across many circles. I started to observe some patterns and traits even among apparently successful people in the current field of work. Soon some of these sessions turned into quasi personal counselling sessions. Some of them took my advice and took a leap of faith towards their dreams. Some kept promising me that they would do it but could never follow through.

I felt a huge sense of responsibility while advising and helping people who took the leap. I did not want my advice to be just generic 'gyaan' and wanted to genuinely help in their new journey. In order to guide them correctly I had to expand my understanding of human behavior and peak performance. It was time to do some thorough work and study the best in the business. My first port of call was my coach, Guru, and mentor—Tony Robbins, the world-renowned personal performance coach. I have had the privilege to be part of six live, intense, multi week programs of Anthony Robbins, or Tony as many of us call him. I had a shelf full of notes and worksheets from many of Tony's programs to fall back on and I spent hours and days revisiting it. I started to read books on resilient entrepreneurs and their habits. Every day, I spent an hour each morning listening to podcasts of business owners, personal performance coaches, athletes, philosophers, and even social observers about facing your fears and pursuing your passion. I met and interviewed people I admire for having chosen a life of their choice, trying to understand their secret sauce.

Finally, I dared to do something new, which is to write a book and share it with people who were sitting at the fence and wanted to do something new but did not have the courage. I wanted to help people like them to give a second shot at life with some logical thought process.

Why will this book benefit you?

This book is not a step-by-step practical guide to succeeding in achieving your dreams. It is not based on any NLP principles or peak performance formula backed by a scientific or psychological study of achieving life's goals and outcomes. This is not a secret code of discovery about the key to avoid failure in your life journey. This book is a gentle nudge for you to start imagining a life of the dreams you are capable of pursuing. This book may act as a springboard for you to execute a plan you have been keeping at the bottom of the shelf and ignored.

This may be a voice of empathy and encouragement to help you face life after your first crash or even the second one. Some of the chapters may deeply resonate with you and could be thought-provoking. Some examples can connect deeply, or some might even have words that may trigger a thought. This book is written to help you overcome limiting beliefs and surpass or conquer a fear of failure. This book may give you the idea to back your own concept. I have arranged my thoughts systematically and logically, but you may avoid following the pattern. Take what makes sense to you and discard what does not. A sincere attempt is to trigger something profound inside you, which may act as an inspiration. It may primarily work like a guardrail or a signpost, like it has already worked for many people. In all honesty, it is all that I hope for from this attempt.

So, are you ready to start something new and give yourself the license to fall?

My sincere and best wishes are with you, and I hope you get the life you deserve.

1
EMBRACING THE UNKNOWN

"Hey Anil, can I skip tomorrow's ride? I'm not very comfortable with the idea of riding a motorcycle in gravel and slush." The man conversing with me was one of the riders on a group tour in the Himalayas that I was leading. I looked at him closely and noticed he was wearing the best possible motorcycle gear that money could buy. He had a machine that had the capability to conquer any kind of terrain. To my understanding, that motorcycle would have burnt an enormous hole in his pocket too. Yet, he was not ready to face the battle. The fear of the unknown was holding him back from exploring new challenges. I gently smiled at him and said, "Don't contemplate too much. Join the ride irrespective of what happens. At any point in time, if you feel you can't do it any further, then stop the bike right there. I'll ensure that the backup van will accompany you back to the base safely."

Quite reluctantly, he joined the ride the following day. To my surprise, he managed to do the entire circuit and enjoyed the process thoroughly. I had no idea that this particular incident changed his life drastically. That very evening around the campfire somewhere in the Himalayas, when we were all sitting together, he walked towards me and said, "Hey, thank you for pushing me. I was terrified of what was ahead. I was afraid of the unknown. I thought I'll fail. In fact, even in my personal life, I generally tend to worry or avoid the unknown. But what you made me do this morning changed my life. I'm going to go back and join my wife in scaling her small business. I'm done with being afraid of the unknown and living my life in perpetual fear."

From that moment, I saw him walking confidently and determinedly. I saw the sparkle of optimism in his eyes to face the world no matter what it offered. It seemed like he had an epiphany. One that let him face his fears. I saw that hunger, to flourish and not live by being scared. His fear was the darkness that prevented him from seeing things from a different angle and exploring new possibilities. A year later, when I spoke with him, I was thrilled to hear that his wife had made significant progress in the business with his active support. Presently, he is a regular guest on our motorcycle tours along with his wife. Apparently, she too has embraced the unknown — of touring on a motorcycle in the lap of the mountains.

"Change is the only constant."— A phrase that we have been spoon-fed since childhood, yet it is something we cannot easily cope with. As humans, we fail to accept change quickly and often contemplate whether we should embrace an unplanned moment or a happening and go with the flow. As individuals, we tend to gravitate towards what is familiar, safe, and comfortable. Our comfort zone is a psychological and emotional space where we feel at ease, free from stress, and in control of our environment. The phrase 'comfort zone' was coined by management thinker Judith Bardwick in her 1991 work *Danger in the Comfort Zone*. Bardwick defines the comfort zone as "a behavioral state where a person operates in an anxiety-neutral position." Brene Brown describes it as "Where our uncertainty, scarcity, and vulnerability are minimized— where we believe we'll have access to enough love, food, talent, time, admiration. Where we feel we have some control."

The concept of the comfort zone goes back to a classic experiment in psychology conducted in 1908 by psychologists Robert M. Yerkes and John D. Dodson. They explained that a state of relative comfort generated a constant level of performance. It was also pointed out that in order to improve that performance, we need to experience a certain level of panic, walk out, and conquer an area in which the stress increases step by step. The psychologists referred to that space as "optimal anxiety" and indicated that it is just outside the boundaries of our comfort zone. Staying within the comfort zone suggests avoiding any sort of uncertainty, which thereby means adopting a passive attitude in life. Well, that feeling of security comes at a price because we miss out on the incentives to live and fall into the tentacles of monotony and apathy. It is precisely the reason why we stick to certain places, patterns, habits, and people, avoiding any factor that introduces novelty because it also gives rise to chaos. Therefore, the comfort zone is a space that we have been conquering but that in turn has also conquered us.

If you look closely, the comfort zone could be the armchair in the drawing room where we prefer to stay instead of going out to explore the world, the work we have been doing for a couple of years, or the tourist destination we return to every year for relaxation. However, within the comfort zone, there isn't a sea of incentives for people to reach new heights of performance. Life is filled with several opportunities, but to grab them, one must leave the boundaries of one's comfort zone. While comfort zones provide a sense of security, they can limit personal growth and the ability fulfill our potential. The comfort zone is an apparent secure place where people can avoid risk, causing their progress to plateau. Most of the time, what holds people back is their frame of mind rather than any distinct lack of knowledge. However, as the old saying goes, "No risk, no gain."— without taking the risk of moving out of the barriers, one cannot gain anything fruitful.

Comfort zones can be a double-edged sword. On the one hand, they offer the stability and predictability necessary for us to function effectively. On the other hand, they can create an invisible barrier that prevents us from exploring new ideas, taking risks, and discovering our true potential. We may miss out on countless opportunities for growth, learning, and success by remaining in our comfort zones. It takes courage for an individual to step out of their comfort zone into the real world, where there are plenty of challenges and hurdles. As the saying goes, "The best sailors aren't born in smooth waters." Without a clear roadmap, there is no way to build on previous experiences. For some, this can provoke anxiety. Hence, they fear walking into the realm of the unknown. However, one must remember that extraordinary things can happen outside the comfort zone. Therefore, it is vital to figure out the right balance in life based on the knowledge of the comfort zone and what can happen if we overcome its limits.

Now, why is it necessary to come out of your comfort zone?
1. To begin with, it contributes to personal growth. The moment you decide to try something new, you give yourself a space to think and learn. When you challenge yourself, you imbibe new skills and gain valuable experiences that contribute to your personal development. When you try to do something,

you have never done before, you might have to restructure a roadmap, pick up new skills, learn new ways of working, or become more flexible. All of these factors can help an individual to grow as a person, be it professionally or personally. However, if one continues to do the same things every single day without any variation, their skillset and behavior can become stagnant, and that will definitely lead to monotony. For example, if you have never tried paragliding before because you are scared of heights, you can choose to slowly face your fear by actually trying it someday. As already mentioned, it is often an irrational fear of the unknown that forbids us from letting ourselves grow, facing our fears, and breaking the shackles.

2. Next it increases your confidence. Do you remember the last time you tried something new? Well, it is very natural that the first time you tried to do it, you may not have aced it. But instead of giving up, if you have tried it repeatedly, you will probably become better at it. This is now a game-changer. Once you shine at something, your confidence around that activity grows and you begin doing even more daring things in order to grow that skill. Overcoming obstacles and facing fears builds self-confidence, empowering you to take on new challenges. Therefore, stepping out of your comfort zone can greatly contribute to growing your confidence. For example, if you are fond of riding motorcycles like me, then probably the

first time you started the vehicle, you were perplexed. You had no idea about what you were doing. You probably stalled it, got nervous, struggled to stay in your lane. However, as time passed, you learned how to ride it better, being more confident and cautious.

3. Walking out of your comfort zone enhances your skills of adaptability. Facing unfamiliar situations teaches you to adapt and thrive in a constantly changing world. One of the critical factors about stepping out of your comfort zone is things can come your way the way you might not expect. This could either be good or bad, a bane or a boon. However, when this happens, you will learn how to adapt to the situation or the outcome and find a manner to make it work in your favor. In this dynamic world, it is vital to understand that not everything will always be in our favor. There will be situations that will make us uncomfortable, anxious, and even scared. However, acquiring the skill of adaptability can help in building the confidence to thrive in any situation or environment. Adaptability is a tremendous positive trait to have as it indicates you are flexible, can roll with the punches, and get accustomed to new environments and situations in a short period of time.

4. It helps in building stronger relationships. When you try out new skills and things or embark on that extra mile to step out of your comfort zone, you are likely to meet new people,

have exciting experiences, come across different ideas that you might not have previously thought of, or receive opportunities that were not previously available to you. When people see you achieving milestones by stepping out of your comfort zone, it will encourage them to see you as an inspiration. People are likely to view you as a confident, energetic, smart individual because in all honesty, it takes guts to leave the comfort zone and walk on the road less travelled, as Robert Frost suggests. Not everyone can have the ability to walk in new directions since no one wants to face the unknown and leave their sense of security. But when you share experiences outside of your comfort zone with others, it can strengthen bonds and create deeper connections.

5. Last, but not the least, coming out of your comfort zone leads to greater creativity. When we stir up our daily schedules, we build our confidence level and allow room for creativity. Having a creative mind builds space to think differently, view things from another perspective, and definitely do things differently. Breaking free from the usual mundane routine and exploring the unknown can fuel your imagination and spark innovative ideas. Staying for too long in the comfort zone can obstruct an individual from developing new skills and even limit career opportunities. The pursuit of creative goals is a part of what makes our lives worth living. By leaving our comfort zone, our brain uses productive stress to help increase

creativity. As one takes small steps towards achieving new things, they become more confident, strong, and adaptable. Being able to set new goals by enhancing your creativity and progressing towards achieving those goals by leaving your comfort zone is undoubtedly a great feeling.

According to Sarah Magnus Sharpe, the Director of Public Relations, and Communications at the Cornell SC Johnson College of Business — *"Leaving the comfort zone inspires motivation and growth."* Developing a skill such as public speaking can be uncomfortable and difficult, but new research shows that instead of avoiding embarrassment, seeking it out can actually result in better motivation and personal growth. Many people find it scary to say a few words in public. Most of the time, people worry about others judging them. People often fear failure. It is this fear that prevents us from exploring new paths. However, keeping the fear of being judged and fear of failure at bay can lead to new opportunities and development in the growth of an individual.

Through the first study and field experiment of its kind at Chicago's Second City, one of the most renowned improvisation clubs in the U.S., Kaitlin Woolley, Associate Professor at the Samuel Curtis Johnson Graduate School of Management, and Ayelet Fishbach, Social psychologist at the University of Chicago, sought to study a way to help people advance challenging goals, such as public speaking. In their paper *"Motivating Personal Growth by Seeking Discomfort,"* published March 29 in Psychological Science, they found that seeking discomfort is motivating because people can tell when they feel uncomfortable, and this "tangible feeling" of discomfort can lead to goal progress. Achieving personal growth often requires experiencing the reality of discomfort. However, instead of tolerating discomfort and awkwardness, one can take a step ahead and actively seek it out. Since discomfort is easy to detect, psychologists suggested that seeking discomfort as a sign of growth can increase motivation. "People often see discomfort as a sign to stop pursuing a goal, yet discomfort often means you are making progress," Woolley said. "We find people can harness discomfort to motivate themselves to achieve important goals."

In general, people aspire to improve themselves and carve a better version of themselves. However, the process of personal growth can be uncomfortable. From building self-confidence to working through difficult emotions to opening oneself to opposing views, self-growth too often evokes discomfort. The progress on personal growth is notoriously difficult to detect. For example, how does an intern know whether they are becoming more confident/excelling during the internship or training process? After getting feedback from the Manager and team members, a trainee can somewhat form an idea of their progress and work on shaping themselves better.

Woolley & Fishbach raises the question— "How can people motivate themselves when experiencing discomfort?" Well, one approach involves reducing the negative experience. For example, people can mentally distance themselves from negative experiences through third-person self-talk. For example, instead of thinking, "Why did I feel this way?" you could instead think, "Why did Anil feel this way?" The moment one distances oneself, one reduces anxiety and thus, improves performance. Another approach involves adding immediate benefits. For example, chocolate ice cream with a cherry on top to counteract discomfort. Wolley and Fishbach have also stated in a study that adding colored pens and snacks has increased high school students' engagement with a math task. Building on cognitive reappraisal research, Woolley and Fishbach ask whether merely encouraging people to seek discomfort can motivate personal growth by transforming discomfort into a sign of progress. For example, in the context of improvisation training, would a person who seeks to feel awkward and uncomfortable be more motivated? In this case, we can only presume that they would.

For their first study, Woolley and Fishbach partnered with the Second City to conduct a multi-wave experiment with more than 550 students across 55 classes. Instructors facilitated the exercise to deliver one of two sets of instructions, either asking students to seek discomfort as their goal (i.e., "your goal is to feel awkward and uncomfortable during the exercise") or baseline instructions that students typically hear when performing an improvised exercise. "Instructing students to seek discomfort increased their persistence and risk-taking in the exercise– they made more progress and learned more," Woolley said. Well, feeling a level of discomfort while pursuing a goal could cause people to reappraise discomfort as the goal progresses. Although personal growth is challenging to detect, people realize when they feel uncomfortable or awkward. People can use this as a cue that they are advancing towards their goal and remain persistent. Although reappraisal interventions traditionally focus on regulating emotion, Woolley & Fishbach proposed that this technique can motivate the pursuit of personal growth and merely be activated by encouraging people to seek discomfort.

In four additional experiments, the researchers found that seeking discomfort is motivating when writing about complex emotional events and learning about health information, such as the COVID-19 pandemic, opening oneself to opposing political viewpoints, and learning about the issue of gun violence. For example, Democrats and Republicans alike were more open to hearing the other party's political views when seeking discomfort, rather than when seeking to learn. "Our society is becoming more politically divided. Our intervention helps open people up to information that is important, but uncomfortable to hear and may help close the political divide," Woolley said.

To conclude the study, the researchers determined that to grow in life and at work, people need to put themselves in situations that may feel daunting, such as pitching a new idea, making a career change, or cold calling. "When we feel out of our comfort zone, we interpret that as a sign to proceed carefully, or not at all. Yet ultimately to succeed in business, we need to take risks," Woolley said. "Seeking discomfort can help ensure our success." Accordingly, their main prediction is that seeking discomfort will motivate personal growth. Instead of seeing discomfort as unrelated to the goal or as a signal to stop, people will start perceiving it as a sign of progress toward their goal.

Now, the ultimate question is: **How do we step out of our comfort zones?**

The **FIRST** step is to start small— Begin with manageable challenges that are slightly outside your comfort zone. Gradually, as time passes, increase the difficulty level when you gain confidence and experience. If you are stuck in a loop, break the pattern. Try to look for spots in your life that feel repetitive or monotonous. Learn to challenge yourself in little ways every day. Look for ways to step outside your comfort zone by taking minimal actions. Once you have stepped out of your comfort zone into a routine, it will be much easier to handle the more significant and far more critical challenges in life. For example, if you always go to the same cafe each time you hang out with your friend, try something else within the same locality. Or, if you are accustomed to wearing yellow at work, try out different colors and see which one works for you. Changing up your usual routine helps bring new experiences into your life. These things may not be gigantic or may not have a deep impact on your life, but you have to start somewhere, little by little.

The **SECOND** step is to create a growth mindset. One must embrace challenges as an opportunity for learning and growth. Contemplate a few things that scare you or make you nervous. You can write them down in a list and put a star next to the one you want to start with. You can tackle the others later. A list helps formulate a plan for how exactly you want to put yourself out there. For example, curate a list that includes "Go skydiving. Write a novel. Join the gym. Start a freelance business . . . and so on." Instead of just thinking about it, you can develop specific ideas that force you to put these plans into action. Only some challenges will lead to success. So, as much as the fear of the unknown creates panic, you must understand that failure is a part of life and not the end of the world. The more you give your mind the space to grow, the more you learn about yourself and gain new experiences. Try to develop a positive attitude towards failure, viewing it as a valuable learning experience.

The **THIRD** step is to set clear goals. Before anything else, clarify who you are and what you want. You need to make a plausible list and define specific, achievable goals that will motivate you to push beyond your comfort zone. Break down significant goals into smaller, manageable steps to make them less daunting. You can think about what you want to gain out of these goals/new experiences. Once you have clarity, write them down on paper and return to the paper each time you want to back out. This can help remind you why you originally wanted to step out of your comfort zone and boost your motivation. You can also research the productivity of your goals to keep yourself well-informed. You will be comfortable trying new things if you are aware of it. This will leave you less confused and can even help you get excited about the change. For example, if you wish to ride to Ladakh on a motorcycle by the end of this summer, research the necessary things to keep in mind while you are on your journey to have a safe and memorable trip. However, make sure the information you find is reputable to ensure you are knowledgeable and prepared.

Going ahead, the **FOURTH** step is to seek support. Do not feel ashamed to reach out for help. It is okay not to know certain things and to not have everything all sorted at once. Therefore, surround yourself with people who encourage your growth, bring out the best in you, and are willing to support you as you take risks. A strong support system can make stepping out of your comfort zone less intimidating. Sometimes, doing something completely new alone can make it even more challenging and intimidating. However, you should take a step ahead and ask for support if needed. It is essential to pick someone who is, for example, naturally adventurous to try new things and learn new experiences. If you set a goal to join the gym, you can bring your friends. Or, if you choose to gain a library membership, bring a buddy along to read books. In this way, you will feel more comfortable navigating the unfamiliar terrain. If you start a new business, ask your friends, ex-colleagues, family members, and other well-wishers to support you in your new venture.

LASTLY, and most importantly— learn to embrace discomfort. No matter what you do, there will always be an anxious situation or a feeling of discomfort when you try something new. You must recognize that discomfort is a natural part of growth and change and not an obstruction to your goal. Hence, learn to embrace and view it as a sign that you are challenging yourself and expanding your boundaries.

Take deep breaths and focus on what you want. As you breathe, picture yourself also taking in confidence. Once this confidence has fueled you up, it is there to stay. Release your breath and your insecurities along with it. This will help you relax and enjoy the challenges that life offers. Thus, it will help in embracing the situation and release discomfort. You can even picture the worst-case scenario to put your discomfort into perspective. Take a deep breath and ask yourself, "What is the worst that could possibly happen?" Think about how you could deal with those circumstances if they really happened. Once you are prepared for the worst, you can only be happily surprised by something better that occurs.

To conclude, I want to ask you— Can you identify the comfort zones you are in regarding your work, relationships, and personal growth?

What are the possible situations that can create anxiety in your mind?

What is stopping you from stepping out of your comfort zone? Do you want to challenge yourself?

Do you want to try something different from what you usually do?

Do you want to make a definite plan with goals and dates to get out of your comfort zone?

Do you want to push your boundaries and grow?

Or are you too comfortable to even attempt?

No matter what, remember that there is not a lot of room for adventure and excitement within your comfort zone. The real journey begins when you leave and face the world alone. To add a little zest to your life and experience personal growth, it is essential to try new things, even if they might look scary or intimidating sometimes. Getting outside of your sense of safety may be tough in the beginning, but facing unfamiliar challenges can make you happier and more fulfilled in the long run. Therefore, stretch your limits. Step out of your comfort zone, embrace the unknown, and expand your horizons of experiences!

2
BEING PREPARED

"If you want to be the best, you have to do things other people aren't willing to do."
−Michael Phelps

As you might have heard, Michael Fred Phelps is widely known as the most phenomenal Olympian of all time, with 28 Olympic medals, out of which 23 are gold, spanning over four Olympic Games. He was born in Towson, Maryland, on June 30, 1985, to his parents— Fred and Debbie Phelps. While being taken for swimming lessons with his two older sisters, Phelps was intimidated as a child to even put his face into water. However, he slowly overcame his discomfort as time faded. In 1996, Michael Phelps was inspired by the performances of Tom Malchow and Tom Dolan during the Olympic Games in Atlanta, Georgia.

As a child, he had an extreme case of attention deficit hyperactivity disorder (ADHD) and was on medication throughout his childhood. He failed to concentrate on anything and struggled dreadfully in school. Despite grappling with an acute case of ADHD, somewhere, Phelps sought solace in swimming when he turned seven. Thus, his mother made it a legitimate routine to take him to swimming classes because it was something he could do alone and enjoy at his own pace. Swimming had given Michael a different outlook on life, and he started to commit to his goal of becoming a great swimmer. For a young lad who struggled with ADHD, the swimming pool was a surprising remedy. "The pool was really good for Michael," his mother explained. Once Phelps moved past his initial hatred of water, the pool became his comfort zone. As Michael said, "In the water, I felt, for the first time, in control." Slowly, with time, it became widely apparent to everyone that Michael was destined for "larger than life" things in his chosen area. After Phelps retired in 2016, he stated, *"The only reason I ever got in the water was my mom wanted me to just learn how to swim. My sisters and I fell in love with the sport, and we decided to swim."*

In the year 2000, Michael Phelps qualified in the 200-meter butterfly race held at Sydney, Australia. At fifteen, he was the youngest male Olympian, which the United States had presented in nearly seventy to eighty years. At the 2003 World

Aquatics Championships, Michael Phelps won four gold medals and two silver medals and broke five world records. During the period between the 2004 and 2008 Olympics, Micheal Phelps amassed a vast number of world records, thoroughly displacing Ian Thorpe as the nucleus of the swimming world. Phelps worked quite closely with his coach, Bob Bowman, to set specific and achievable goals for each season. These goals were broken down into smaller, manageable objectives, allowing Phelps to focus on incremental improvements. By continuously setting and achieving these smaller milestones, Phelps was able to build a foundation for long-term success. Well, the quote by Phelps that marks the beginning of this chapter is not about how to win a swimming race, but on how to prepare for it.

The difference between a great swimmer and the most outstanding athlete ever in Olympic history was in the rigorous preparation that Michael Phelps put himself through. According to Bowman, Michael Phelps swam 13 kilometers a day, six or seven days a week— at least 80,000 meters every week, including Sundays and birthdays. He split his training into two consecutive sessions, spending five to six hours in the pool daily. The dedication, intensity, and volume in training was astonishing— swimming 80,000 meters a week, consuming 8000 calories per day, ice baths that lasted for five minutes, working out at the gym for hours, functional training with weights thrice a week, training in different types of water, getting regular massages, adequate sleep, hours of mental visualization each week and so on. The incredulous list of preparation was never-ending. The commitment and torture he was willing to put himself through, made each Olympic medal almost like a walk in the park for Michael. The truth is that he had won them much before the swimming race even began. Yes, this is the epitome of what preparedness can be for the highest goal post by the world's greatest living sportsperson. You may not need to go to this extreme while preparing for your goals and challenges. However, some level of preparedness is a must.

Before I start any motorcycle tour, either solo or a group ride, I start my preparation weeks in advance. I begin with route planning by researching the route, road conditions, likely weather, the best lunch, and coffee stops, etc. Not only this, I even research emergency services like medical services available enroute. After that, I prepare myself by getting ready for the long and arduous journey ahead. I get myself in better shape and focus on areas especially my back which has been my 'Achilles heel' for a long time. I start working with my physio to strengthen specific muscles and improve my diet. Then, I begin concentrating on my riding gear. Depending on where I am headed, I start packing the right kind of riding gear to ensure they are in good condition for the tour. Thoroughly inspecting the gear to ensure that there are no surprises of malfunctioning while on the tour has almost become a ritual for me. I also build my mental resilience by pushing myself to train in smaller versions of rough terrains that I could possibly encounter. Finally, I shift my focus to the machine. I send my motorcycle to the authorized service center and examine it thoroughly on all the vital functioning parts. Even after it comes back from the service station, I do one last round of personal inspection to ensure that no loose nuts or bolts may come in the way of a smooth tour. In short, it is like a war preparation that I go through to undertake a tour. I spend more time preparing for the ride than the time I spend on the actual ride itself. Life has taught me that if I do not spend time preparing, I will invariably end up paying for it while on the tour. I am a huge believer in the theory that 'planning time should be greater than the event in itself'.

Now, the question is— Why is it important to prepare thoroughly?

Well, the first perk of being well-prepared is that it helps you build confidence. When you are aware and well-prepared, you are more likely to feel confident in your skills and abilities. Confidence is crucial in high-stakes situations, as it allows you to trust your training and perform without hesitation or doubt. Projecting confidence helps individuals gain credibility, deal with pressure, and tackle personal and professional challenges.

For example, you want to start a Cloud Kitchen but have not understood yet the intricacies of cold chain logistics. In that case, it is likely that you will feel under confident and anxious about scaling the business. On the other hand, if you have thoroughly invested time and effort by acquiring knowledge in areas of business where you have much less understanding or exposure, you will feel a lot more ready. Therefore, by focusing on preparation, you instill a belief in yourself and your abilities, ultimately contributing to better performance.

The next benefit of being well prepared is that it helps you identify your weakness and provides opportunities for improvement. When you figure out your strengths and weaknesses you give yourself enough room to build on your skills. Preparation is an ongoing process that involves continuously evaluating your performance, identifying areas for improvement, and refining your skills. This iterative approach ensures you are constantly growing and evolving, making you better equipped to face new challenges and succeed in your chosen field. For example, if you realize that you get anxious while public speaking or are afraid to share your opinions in a group project, you should prioritize working on your speaking skills. Once you identify and accept your drawbacks, it will be convenient for you to put your effort in the right places.

One of the biggest things that comes with being prepared is mental preparedness. Mental preparation is a critical component of overall preparation. Visualization, meditation, and other mental training techniques help you develop a strong mindset and stay focused under pressure. With a strong mindset, you can avoid other temptations and distractions that can hinder your progress. Once you visualize yourself attaining a specific goal, you are halfway on that path. For example, imagine you are overweight, and your doctor has given you a strict diet and exercise to maintain a healthy lifestyle and lose the excess fat. Given how we live in a world surrounded by junk food, it is fairly understandable if you get tempted. However, the real deal lies here— To choose what is best for you and mentally prepare yourself to reach that position. Nothing can make you sway once you fix your mind to maintain a healthy, balanced diet, no matter what hardships you face. Therefore, by prioritizing mental preparation, you can harness the power of your mind to overcome obstacles and perform at your peak.

Every individual should prepare themselves thoroughly as it minimizes the impact of external factors. On the actual day, countless external factors such as weather, unforeseen circumstances, or even how you feel physically can impact your performance. By placing a greater emphasis on preparation, you reduce the influence of these external factors and increase your chances of success. There have been times when, despite being well-prepared to ace my motorcycle trip, some external factors arose to jeopardize situations. But no matter what obstacle came up, be it unforeseen weather conditions, sudden ill-health, or anything for that matter, I found ways to overcome them because I was well-prepared for the trip. Well, the confidence to combat any situation cannot arise out of the blue. It takes a lot of preparation, hard work, focus, and more importantly, the determination to reach the desired goal.

Lastly, one of the significant things that being well-prepared bestows on you with is long-term success. Preparation is undoubtedly the foundation for long-term success. By focusing on the process and dedicating yourself to continuous improvement, you create a strong foundation that enables you to reach new heights in your career or sport. In contrast, relying solely on the big day is a short-sighted approach that may lead to temporary success but will not provide a sustainable path to greatness. As H. Jackson Brown Jr. says, *"The best preparation for tomorrow is doing your best today."* Unless you give your 100% today, you cannot expect fruitful results tomorrow. When you read through the first few pages of this chapter, you came to know a lot about Michael Phelps. Do you think he would have been widely regarded as the greatest of all time (GOAT) had he just focused on the days of the swimming competition? Phelps would not have acquired 28 Olympic gold medals had he not prepared himself for such a long journey. It takes years of hard work, dedication, resilience, discipline to reach your final destination.

Benjamin Franklin says, *"By failing to prepare, you are preparing to fail."* Once the water has run downstream, you cannot get it back. Similarly, when you have no clue about how you reach your goal, unprepared, you lose the opportunity, squandering the moment. Preparation is the cornerstone of peak performance. It is what allows you to perform at your best on the actual day, regardless of external factors or unavoidable circumstances. By dedicating yourself to consistent practice, mental training, and ongoing self-improvement, you will not only be better prepared for the big day but also build a foundation for long-term success. As the saying goes, *"Planning leads to awareness. Preparation leads to readiness."* Life is spontaneous, and there are countless things that take us by surprise that we never see coming.

However, I also firmly believe in being flexible and not trying to control everything or being too rigid about things because even the kind of fall you have can be tempered by the level of preparedness. Like in motorcycling, veteran riders can teach novices the fine art of falling or the preparedness to fall with least damage to self and motorcycle as an essential skill. This also dictates how quickly we can jump to a different plan if needed or practice flexibility and adapt when situations change.

When we routinely prepare ourselves for anything we desire, we enhance our self-discipline. I am sure you have come across this quote by Abraham Lincoln— *"If I had eight hours to chop down a tree, I'd spend six hours sharpening my axe."* People who have confidence in themselves and are well-prepared have a significant advantage over any obstacles they encounter. I agree that we cannot be prepared for everything in life, which comes with its probability of eccentricity. But we can always prepare for things that are fairly expected to occur. In my opinion, self-discipline is one of the foundations of living a blissful life. The act of becoming prepared indicates that we discipline ourselves to make the time to prepare. Thus, we get over the feeling of "I don't feel like doing this now" and put off procrastination. We consciously dump the excuses and become mindful of what we are doing and ourselves.

So, how do you embrace the power of preparation and unlock your full potential?

The very **FIRST** thing to keep in mind is to have a strategic plan. Ideally, without proper planning, you will not have a direction to move forward. Therefore, it is vital to set goals and create a roadmap to reach that mark. The first step in any journey is to define your destination. Your goals should be specific, measurable, achievable, relevant, and time-bound (SMART). Being specific gives you a clear direction, enough space for tracking progress, keeps you grounded, ensures alignment with your larger vision, and the time-bound nature adds a sense of urgency. Once your goals are set, strategic planning is the next step. Strategic planning offers a plethora of benefits which can significantly contribute to long-term success. It will improve your decision-making skills that align with the mission and vision. It will also ensure that all actions and initiatives are driven towards its defined goals. This involves breaking down your larger goals into smaller, manageable tasks and setting a timeline. The detailed roadmap helps maintain focus, manage time effectively, and build momentum as you tick off completed tasks. If you are self-disciplined and open to planning strategically, your thought processes will expand with fluidity and flexibility.

The **SECOND** step towards embracing the power of preparation is prioritizing your tasks. Not all tasks are created equally. Some tasks will have a higher impact on your goals than others. In today's world, it is pretty convenient to fall into the trap of being "too busy chasing cows to build a fence." To overcome a pattern of spending all day "chasing cows," you can outsource, batch small tasks, eliminate unimportant tasks, and streamline your workflow. As human beings, there is so much that we desire to accomplish in our personal and professional lives. Thus, we must decide which goals to tackle first. You must prioritize tasks based on their urgency and importance. Establishing priorities is mandatory to complete everything that needs to be done. Prioritization is essential because it will allow you to divide your attention into important and urgent tasks so that you can later focus on lower-priority tasks. For each goal, decide how long you would like to spend time on it and when and when you would like to achieve it. This will ensure that you are focusing on activities that bring you closer to your goals, rather than getting caught up in less significant tasks. If you do not take the time to prioritize, then you will have trouble getting things done on time and later stress about how you will finish everything on your to-do list. For example, you have been given an assignment at your workplace, and its due date is tomorrow. Now, instead of prioritizing on getting it done, if you choose to watch Netflix, then you are likely to get reprimanded by your boss in no time.

The **THIRD** thing to keep in mind is to cultivate proactivity. Proactivity is about taking initiative and anticipating future needs or changes. This mindset allows you to seize opportunities and mitigate potential challenges. For some people, the day-to-day scramble might be a great source of energy and motivation, but it can be difficult to sustain over a long-term career trajectory. Being reactive can make it difficult to create boundaries, to make time for reflection, or to re-evaluate what you are doing and where you want to be. Therefore, the antidote to reactivity is indeed proactivity. One must set aside time for preparation and hone one's preferences for career longevity. To cultivate proactivity, practice anticipating outcomes, foreseeing potential obstacles, and preparing contingency plans. Regularly revisit and adjust your plans to stay aligned with your goals. Being proactive indicates willingly initiating behavior that addresses issues before they barge out of the blue. The opposite of being proactive is to be reactive, in which you respond to events after they occur. For example, an individual who is proactive about their health is likely to maintain a healthy, balanced diet, exercise, take preventive measures, and go for frequent checkups. On the contrary, a reactive person might perform the same actions only after being instructed by a doctor. The proactive person works toward achieving a goal that inherently avoids unpleasant circumstances, whereas the reactive person first encounters an unwanted circumstance before devising a positive goal.

 I believe that building consistency is the key to achieving long-term goals. Therefore, the **FOURTH** point is to consistently focus on your goals. It is about showing up and doing the work, day after day, regardless of how motivated you feel. Consistency is the critical driver for success. Being consistent means devoting yourself to your goals and being focused on them daily. It requires a long-term commitment from you and involves sustained effort in performing actions repeatedly. Discipline, accountability and responsibility are non-negotiable if you prefer to consistently accomplish your dreams and desires. Being consistent and dedicated in your journey can help you succeed in any field you embark on. Building routines and habits that support your goals can help ensure consistency.

Remember— It is better to make steady, incremental progress than to seek quick, unsustainable results. As Dwayne Johnson aka THE ROCK says, *"Success isn't always about greatness. It's about consistency. Consistent hard work leads to success. Greatness will come."* Any individual who has tried to achieve a demanding goal knows consistency is critical. Whether working out in the gym, eating healthy, working for a project, or studying for an exam, there is no substitute for consistency. Well, the reason is simple— Consistency leads to momentum. The more consistently you focus on something, the easier it becomes, and the more momentum you build up. Eventually, what was once a dreadful struggle becomes a habit, and we all know that habits are hard to break. Therefore, consistency is undeniably essential and is the key to making lasting change.

The **LAST STEP** towards unlocking your full potential is evaluating your progress. If you regularly assess your progress toward your goals, it will help you understand whether your current strategies are effective or if adjustments are needed. Setting personal and professional goals can increase your productivity and give a sense of gratification, but measuring your progress is essential to setting an effective goal. It can also help you to identify how to adjust your plan of action, which may speed up your progression. After placing an effective goal, measuring your progress can help you understand what actions contribute to your progress and which methods are most beneficial. After proper scrutiny, you can incorporate these methods into your overall strategy for accomplishing your dreams. Celebrate your successes, learn from your failures, and use these insights to refine your approach. For example, if a student aims to pass an exam with a high score, they may use a calendar to clarify the test date and establish a study deadline. Then, they may outline topics they are weak in to estimate how much time to spend studying each day and set milestones to stay focused. They would make it a point to see where they stand and put more effort into the areas where they are weak.

Planning and proactivity are potent tools in achieving your goals, however big or small. It will give you the confidence to embark on uncharted territories and face obstacles while on the path. Always remember that the journey to achieving your goals is a marathon, not a sprint, and these strategies will keep you moving forward, one step at a time. Whether aiming to climb the career ladder, save up for a vacation or adventurous activities, having a solid plan in advance can bridge the difference between achieving your objectives and falling short. An effective plan helps break complex goals into smaller, manageable pieces and anticipate potential risks before pushing forward with any strategy. Being proactive is distinctive and essential because, most of the time, what we do is dictated by past habits, current circumstances, and pressures. By knowing the power of action to achieve results, you can focus on changing yourself for the better. You can target your own behavior - for example, strengthening your leadership tactics, speaking skills, work habits, job performance or overall health. Planning and proactivity provide a clear path forward, keep you focused on what is important, and empower you to navigate challenges and seize opportunities.

Take a moment now to consider how you usually go about your daily life. Are you missing out on some exciting opportunities because you are not preparing yourself sufficiently? Do you end up repeating the same "mistakes" because you resist preparation? If yes, then think about all the benefits of being well prepared that you extracted from this chapter. Like Michael Phelps, you would have already won the race before the race even began. So, think about the dream that you want to chase. Think about all your unfulfilled desires. Take a step today. Keep your insecurities at bay. This is the moment. Do not waste time and give your way to procrastination and self-doubt. Seize the day. Set clear goals that you wish to accomplish within a deadline. Create a strategic plan to achieve those goals. Spend more time preparing before you even take one physical step towards it. Follow your dreams consistently and keep track of your progress.

I promise you that the energy and the confidence you will feel will be totally different than when you once thought about it. Start preparing now, and you will be halfway through your final destination. And in case, if you ever doubt your potential, remember the words of Michael Phelps, *"When I said I wanted to win eight gold medals, basically half the people in the swimming world thought I was absolutely crazy, and nobody could ever do something like that. But for me, I was somebody who believed in it and somebody who believed in the process of getting there. I knew it wasn't going to happen overnight... but every small thing we did was a small steppingstone in order to have that chance and that opportunity to do what I did in 2008. From 2002 to 2008, it was basically trial and error."*

3
CALCULATED RISKS AND TRUSTING YOUR INSTINCTS

"There are only two types of riders— the one who had a fall and the one who is about to fall," a fellow rider and good friend once said. Reflecting on it later, I realized it is so true. Every motorcyclist has a story of a fall, but still, most of us never stop riding. When I think of it, motorcycling is one endeavor full of risks at every stage. You may be living in a vast city, or you may be living in a small village. There could be dozens of hazards that you have to successfully overcome every time you take out your machine for a ride. This is vehemently true for someone who rides for pleasure or as a commuter. The motorcyclist takes a series of calculated risks every day, which has a high probability of succeeding while reaching his destination. The ability to take calculated risks every day makes a motorcyclist/

two-wheeler rider an expert in one aspect of life. In fact, I strongly believe that risks are the ultimate proof that our dreams are great and real.

If you take a look at Elon Musk's journey, you will notice how it has been a series of well-thought-out and calculated risks. He was born in 1971 in South Africa; Musk moved to the United States for his studies. His entrepreneurial journey started in college, where he and his brother Kimbal started a company called Zip2 with a loan from their father. Zip2 was a city guide software for newspapers, sold to Compaq for approximately $300 million in 1999. Musk used his share of the sale to co-found X.com, which later became PayPal, the online payments company. PayPal was sold to eBay for $1.5 billion in 2002. After the sale of PayPal, instead of resting on his laurels, Musk took another significant risk by investing his money into three ambitious startups— SpaceX, Tesla, and SolarCity. SpaceX was founded to reduce the cost of space travel and explore the possibility of making Mars a future home for humans.

The company faced numerous challenges and failures in the beginning. In fact, the first three launches of the SpaceX Falcon 1 rocket failed to reach orbit. After spending $100 million of his own money, Musk was on the verge of bankruptcy. Despite these setbacks, the fourth launch in September 2008 was successful. In the same year, SpaceX won a $1.6 billion contract with NASA to resupply the International Space Station. In the same way Elon Musk faced significant challenges with Tesla. The company almost went bankrupt in 2008, during the Great Recession. Musk decided to invest his own money to keep the company afloat. His calculated risk paid off when the company's first electric car, the Roadster, became a run-away success against the predictions of auto pundits. Ever since then, Tesla has become a leader in electric vehicle technology. SolarCity— a solar energy services company, was also a risky venture. Musk served as the chairperson of the company, which faced significant financial difficulties. In a controversial move in 2016, Tesla acquired SolarCity. Despite criticism and financial stress, Musk remained persistent. Today, the company is a significant player in the renewable energy sector. Elon Musk's entrepreneurial journey is characterized by his willingness to invest in high-risk and high-reward scenarios. He had failures along the way, but his successes have significantly impacted several industries, ranging from financial services to automotive to space travel and renewable energy.

The concept of calculated risk is often stated but seldom understood in detail. In the pursuit of success, one often encounters moments that require a leap of faith. Taking risks is an essential part of growth and progress. However, there is a distinct difference between taking blind risks and calculated risks. Calculated risk is often defined as "A carefully considered decision that exposes a person to a degree of personal and financial risk that is counterbalanced by a reasonable possibility of benefit." Calculated risks refer to thoughtfully assessed actions that involve a certain degree of uncertainty but are supported by a careful evaluation of potential outcomes, costs, and benefits. They involve a systematic process of gathering information, analyzing variables, and making informed decisions. Rather than impulsive gambles, calculated risks are strategic moves aimed at maximizing opportunities while minimizing potential downsides. When it comes to risk-taking, the prevailing sentiment seems to be "just take a leap of faith that it will work out." After all, didn't Bill Gates and Steve Jobs drop out of college to pursue their dreams? Although they dropped out and found massive success at Microsoft and Apple, one should pay attention to the hard work, planning, and preparation that went into taking the risks they signed up for.

There are vital differences between blind risks and calculated risks. Our willingness to take risks (avoidable or unavoidable), our ability to wait or the speed in decision making are central features of our personality. However, impulsive risks may not always be fruitful in the long run. Blind risks are impulsive actions taken without thorough analysis or considering potential consequences. They often arise from emotional or impulsive decisions and lack a comprehensive understanding of the situation. Calculated risks involve weighing the likelihood of success or failure of a particular decision.

On the contrary, blind risks involve ignoring or underestimating the potential for failure. Calculated risks consider the potential consequences of a particular decision, be it positive or negative. On the other hand, blind risks involve a disregard for the possible consequences of an action. In general, bind risks are akin to playing the lottery, relying heavily on luck and chance. However, calculated risks are rooted in knowledge, experience, and careful assessment. They involve a clear understanding of the risks involved, potential rewards, and mitigation strategies in case of setbacks. When it comes to taking risks, one must trust their gut. Sadly, too many people confuse a gut instinct with fear. It is human nature to overestimate the possibility of failure and underestimate our own abilities to thrive in life. Well, it is the fear that is murmuring, and it can be immobilizing. However, sitting idle and doing nothing is a risk and can be just as destructive to your emotional and financial well-being as risks taken recklessly.

Now, why is it important to take calculated risks?

Well, before delving into the factors, we must keep Mark Zuckerberg's quote in mind— *"The biggest risk is not taking any risk. In a world that's changing really quickly, the only strategy that is guaranteed to fail is not taking risks."* The very first factor to keep in mind is that calculated risks enable your scope for growth. Do you ever look back at your life and wish that you had taken a different path? Most people are afraid to choose the riskier option because of what could have happened if they had made certain decisions. But if you face your fear and embrace the unknown, you will grow as a person. For example, you may fear skydiving as it is risky because your parachute might not open at the right time, and you could end up splattered in a field amongst terrified cattle, etc. But what if nothing goes wrong? What if everything goes smoothly as planned and you turn out to be victorious in the end? One of the best ways to combat negative emotions is to actually trust your instincts for a while and just go with the flow. Calculated risks push individuals and organizations beyond their comfort zones, fostering growth and innovation. By stepping into the unknown, we challenge ourselves to learn, adapt, and develop new skills, ultimately leading to personal and professional growth.

The second factor is that calculated risks give you space to seize opportunities. People are very keen to "be safe in the comfort zone" these days, but there is no such thing as real safety. To live an authentic life, one is required to throw oneself off proverbial cliffs and discover whether one will sink or swim. Calculated risk-takers recognize that opportunity often lies just beyond the threshold of uncertainty. There are several people who have fallen into deep pits of depression because they haven't got the job they desired, nor attained the goals they aimed for, simply because they were too afraid of rejection and failure. Let us say, for example, you have chosen to give a speech at an event. Despite knowing that you have social anxiety, if you trust yourself a bit and go for it instead of worrying about who will judge you or if you will fail, you might end up acing your speech and can completely overcome your fear of public speaking. It can even open several doors for you in the future. By embracing calculated risks, individuals position themselves to seize opportunities that others may overlook or shy away from. These opportunities can propel them toward success and open new avenues for advancement.

Lastly, calculated risks help in overcoming fear and building resilience. As already stated, fear is one of the biggest obstacles to taking risks. The fear of failure, fear of the unknown, and fear of drifting away from our comfort zone can hold us back from achieving our goals. When we take calculated risks, we allow ourselves to evaluate the potential outcomes and make rational decisions. Failure is an inevitable part of taking any kind of risk. At the same time, failure can also be a valuable learning experience and help you build resilience. When we take calculated risks, we are able to learn from our mistakes and make better choices in the future. For example, if you are a chef trying to open your own restaurant, taking a calculative risk might involve investing a significant amount of money. If customers do not like your dishes, you can learn from experience and make the necessary changes to your strategy, moving forward and attracting more clients. Taking calculated risks allows individuals to confront their fears, build resilience, and develop a proactive mindset. By embracing uncertainty, individuals become better equipped to handle setbacks, learn from failures, and adapt to changing circumstances.

Elon Musk says, *"If things are not failing, you are not innovating enough."* Taking calculated risks is an imperative part of personal and professional growth. By taking risks, we can achieve our goals, learn from failure, and build confidence in our abilities. By following a deliberate and thoughtful approach to making decisions, people can take calculated risks that provide opportunities for success and individual growth. Life often presents us with challenges, setbacks, and obstacles that may seem insurmountable. However, it is those people who possess certain qualities that can defy the odds and achieve remarkable success by taking calculated risks.

Now, what are those 'certain' qualities?

The **BIGGEST** unavoidable factor is courage. Well, it takes courage to bet against the odds. It means stepping outside of our comfort zones and venturing into the unknown. Courage enables us to face our fears head-on and embrace uncertainty with unwavering determination. The first time James Bond, Jack Reacher, or Lara Croft let go and went in a new direction, they probably experienced enormous fear. However, by having indomitable courage and overriding that fear, they were able to create a new definition of what is possible. For example, let's say you have a job interview today, and there are several renowned candidates from reputed institutes. Let's say you have above-average academic qualifications. While it is expected to feel a little overwhelmed, you will emerge victorious if you have the courage and confidence to give your best without fearing the results. As we know, it is not called "mission: impossible" for nothing. Courage is the driving force that propels us forward when the odds are stacked against us. Without courage, we may never take that leap of faith necessary to achieve greatness. The reason some people achieve great things is that they are prepared to test their risk limitations and have boundless courage to take the road less taken.

The **SECOND** quality to defy all odds is the sheer amount of resilience. To bet against the odds, one must be resilient. Setbacks and failures are inevitable along the journey, but the ability to bounce back, learn from mistakes, and persevere sets apart the victorious. Resilience allows us to view obstacles as opportunities for growth rather than insurmountable barriers. The barriers can help us develop a growth mindset and build resilience to overcome future obstacles. It fuels our determination to keep going, even in the face of adversity, and empowers us to rise above challenges with renewed vigor.

For example, if you are a swimmer trying to reach a new level of performance, taking a calculated risk might involve pushing yourself to your limits and competing against tougher opponents. Or say, you are a fresher in a new firm and have been responsible for handling a project. In the beginning it may seem intimidating to you but if you take a leap of faith and go with the flow, do your research, and give your best shot, then that is worthwhile. While you may not always win, these experiences can help you build the resilience necessary to continue pushing yourself and improving over the course of time.

The **THIRD** quality that can help us succeed is adaptability and perseverance. When we face challenges or setbacks, we learn to adapt and persevere. In a world that is constantly evolving, adaptability is crucial when betting against the odds.

It is the willingness to embrace change, be flexible in our approach, and adjust our strategies as needed. Things will not always go as planned. In fact, the universe will always have its own way of surprising you. Therefore, if you have the confidence to adapt yourself to any situation, then that is the real deal. The ability to adapt allows us to navigate unexpected twists and turns, seize new opportunities, and overcome unforeseen challenges. Without adaptability, we risk being left behind, while those who can adapt thrive in the face of uncertainty. The road to victory is rarely smooth, and perseverance is what keeps us going when the odds seem stacked against us. It is the unwavering determination to continue pushing forward, even when faced with seemingly insurmountable obstacles. Perseverance enables us to weather the storms, endure hardships, and stay committed to our goals. Through perseverance, we find the strength to keep fighting, never losing sight of our ultimate objective.

To add further, one must have a clear vision to reach their final destination. Having a clear vision is another essential quality when betting against the odds. It is the ability to see beyond the present circumstances and envision a brighter future. A vision provides us with a sense of purpose and direction, guiding our actions and decisions. Crafting a vision for yourself is foundational to your goal-achievement process. For example, you want to go on the Everest basecamp trek, but you have done zero planning on the itinerary and equipment that you need to carry with you. Will you be able to enjoy the trek? No, right? Instead, if you have a clear vision (plan) of the trip and strategize it according to your preference, you are bound to have an amazing trek.

As Michael Hyatt, author, and former CEO of Thomas Nelson, explains, *"Vision and strategy are both important. But there is a priority to them. Vision always comes first. Always. If you have a clear vision, you will eventually attract the right strategy. If you don't have a clear vision, no strategy will save you."* With a compelling vision in mind, we can chart our course, make strategic choices, and overcome the obstacles that stand in our way. Creating a roadmap will help you stay focused and on the right path to achieve all your goals. It helps you to avoid detours, such as distractions, as well as guards you against potential hazards. A strong vision inspires us to think forward and not focus on past regrets or mistakes. Therefore, a strong vision acts as a beacon of hope and motivation, driving us towards victory.

Finally, the **LAST** quality that one must always possess is innovation. To bet against the odds, innovation is a vital quality that will help an individual remain creative and open to imagination. It is the ability to think outside the box, challenge conventional wisdom, and find creative solutions to problems. Innovation allows us to disrupt the status quo, discover new approaches, and seize untapped opportunities. For example, if you are going to give a PowerPoint presentation at a school and the electricity suddenly goes down, do not feel disheartened. If you can narrate the presentation in a storytelling format, it will catch the attention of the class. You have to be innovative about skills to beat any odd situation.

By embracing innovation, we can turn the odds in our favor, breaking free from the limitations imposed by traditional thinking and charting our own path to success. In general, big dreams take a certain amount of time to achieve. They involve a lot of grit, patience, hard work, and overcoming obstacles. Taking calculated risks can drive innovation. When we take such risks, we are able to explore new ideas and ways of doing things. It can lead to the development of new products, services, and processes that can transform industries and change the world.

In conclusion, to beat against the odds and emerge victorious in life, we must possess qualities such as courage, resilience, vision, adaptability, perseverance, and innovation. These qualities empower us to take calculated risks, face adversity head-on, and navigate the unpredictable terrain of life. By embracing these qualities, we can defy the odds, overcome challenges, and achieve extraordinary success. So, let us cultivate these qualities within ourselves and encourage others to do the same, for it is with these qualities that we can turn the tables and emerge triumphant in the face of any adversity.

You should never forget— there is no success without failure. When we make a misstep at something, we must try again until we get it right and learn an extraordinary amount in the process. I don't know about you, but I would rather risk and fail miserably than spend forever wondering what might have been if I had actually had the courage to try. If you ever feel demotivated or too scared to take any risk, remember the words of Israelmore Ayivor, the CEO and founder of Moretalks— *"To become a better you, dare to take calculated risks and overcome your limitations. Your scars can make you a star, but you have to decide."*

4
FOCUS ON THE JOURNEY, NOT THE DESTINATION

If you are acquainted with Indian mythology, I guess you might have had the opportunity to come across the legendary saint—Maharishi Agastya. At a certain point, he told two of his favorite disciples to undertake a journey of over a hundred miles to the top of a sacred mountain to receive the ultimate 'gift' kept at its summit. They left with the notion that this 'gift' shall complete their learning, and they will be ready to become a wise seer like him once they reach the summit and receive the gift. The two disciples set for the journey, which was a long and arduous one, passing many small villages, farmlands, dense forests, and rivers on the way. As they continued the journey, they faced rough weather, like torrential rain and scorching heat. After almost two weeks of the difficult journey, the weary disciples reached the summit to find no gift awaiting them. They searched high and low to see if their Guru had left anything behind for them.

All of a sudden, they found the great saint walking towards them out of the blue. The great Sage noticed that one of the disciples looked more disappointed than the other. He asked both of them about their journey and what they saw on the way here. The first disciple mentioned that he was so focused on reaching the summit that he was not distracted by any sights and sounds on the way. He said he braved the weather and the hardships with a precise determination to reach the summit in order to receive the gift. The other disciple sheepishly replied that he could not help but notice several things on the way. The saint asked him, "What did you see on the way here?" and the disciple replied, saying, "I saw the beautiful countryside life and the wonderful people living in peace. I couldn't help but notice the generosity of the people, although they had very little with themselves. I found that people were living in harmony with nature and took good care of their pets and farm animals. I realized that the less they have, the more content they are." Maharishi Agastya smiled and said, "I see you have found your gift already."

The biggest reason why I feel people should focus on the journey and not the destination is because happiness is found not in finishing an activity but in doing it. Life is a journey where we are the traveler and being a traveler inspires you to earn innumerable things throughout your journey. When you focus solely on trying to achieve your goals, it becomes unlikely that you will succeed at the highest level. You might achieve momentary success, but it will not last for long. It will seem like the winds of change, tempestuous one moment, then dying down another moment, because you did not enjoy the journey. If you stay too fixated on reaching your destination instead of enjoying the beauty which the journey offers, you are likely to feel lost. If we remain focused on the destination that we have in our minds, we do not allow ourselves the flexibility and openness to enjoy the mirth and beauty and accept necessary detours that might alter our destination in the end.

Public relations executive and a partner of the European Consultancy Network, Peter Hagerty quotes, *"Life is a journey, and if you fall in love with the journey, you will be in love forever."* Well, this may be the reason why thousands of motorcyclists like me jump on the saddle and embark on long and arduous journeys to unknown places. It is never about the final destination but the entire journey that lures us to undertake these rides. Ask anyone why they ride, and you will get the answers ranging from the feeling of freedom, the people they meet on their way, the feeling of the 'wind in my hair', the thrill and adrenaline rush of traveling around clustered labyrinths, etc. It is never about the final destination. It is always about the journey. Thus, it becomes a passion, an addiction— something that makes you feel alive, something that calms your chaos.

Most motorcyclists I know develop a zen-like faculty over time. They 'live in the moment' and are 'present' while on a motorcycle and seemingly fully immerse themselves in the process. Being present in the moment is the key to staying positive, healthy, and happy. It helps you fight anxiety, eradicate your worries and rumination, and keeps you grounded and connected to your inner self. As a rider on two wheels in India, you need to really be alert at all times; being 'present' is at a different level. It is the state of being fully immersed in the experience and soaking up everything that comes your way. It is a multi-sensorial thing that develops over time— The more you ride, the more present you are. It probably explains why veteran riders are a very interesting lot to hang out with due to their Zen state and the stories about the journey. As the author Myrko Thum shapes it, the present moment is all there truly is: *"The present moment is the only thing where there is no time. It is the point between past and future. It is always there and it is the only point we can access in time. Everything that happens, happens in the present moment. Everything that ever happened and will ever happen can only happen in the present moment. It is impossible for anything to exist outside of it."*

In the golden annals of human history, there are infinite myriad tales of folks who dared to dream big, initially started small but eventually made it large. If you lean closer, you will realize that the most engaging and inspiring part of their stories was the journey, not the arrival. The tale of climbing the mountain rather than the view from the top. The phrase, "Focus on the journey, not the destination," is not a motivational jingle. It is a guiding compass for those who want to engage with life truly. When you cling on to the final result, you limit your satisfaction and deprive yourself of happiness to a specific point. Crossing the "end game" does bring multitudes of joy, but it is always the memories of the journey that you will latch on to.

If you take a look at J.K. Rowling's life— the author of the beloved Harry Potter series did not have it easy. Rowling began writing her first book on welfare as a single mother, juggling the responsibilities of parenthood with her ambition to create an extraordinary story. It was not the prospect of becoming a best-selling author that kept her going through countless rejections and challenges. Instead, it was the sheer joy of crafting a magical universe and the passion of putting her imagination to paper. The journey was her salvation, her muse, and ultimately, her glory. The outcome was just the add-on bonus. As you see, life is not a simple game of connect-the-dots where the sole aim is to get from one point to another. It is more like a grand, thrilling roller coaster ride with unexpected turns, ups, and downs. It is all about experiencing the thrill of the ride and marveling at the views as you zoom past the breeze. At this point, you might ask, "Why does focusing on the journey matter?" Focusing on the journey radiates a light on what else you get from trying to reach your goals. The journey is where you see, learn, and evolve. In some ways, achieving goals is just a by-product of your journey.

Now, why do you think the journey is more important than the destination?

First, the journey teaches us valuable lessons. When we embark on a journey, we will encounter challenges and obstacles. These challenges may seem daunting at first, but they can teach us important things that we can carry with us for the rest of our lives. We learn how to solve problems, be resilient, and adapt to new situations. These skills are not only useful at the moment but can also be applied to other areas of our lives. When you go through several things during a journey, it is natural to introspect and realize what you are doing right and where you might go wrong. You could reflect on the experience after you reach your final destination, but you can also do so while you are trying to get there. Focusing on the journey helps individuals develop a broad mindset and sharpen their perspectives on life.

Second, the journey allows us to grow as individuals. As we face challenges and overcome obstacles, we grow as individuals. We become stronger, more confident, and more self-aware. We learn about our strengths and weaknesses and how to leverage them to achieve our goals. This growth is not limited to the journey itself but can also continue long after reaching our destination. In fact, when we work tirelessly to achieve something, the satisfaction and plethora of happiness that we receive when we finally lay our hands on it is inexplicable. As the journey becomes complex and more challenging, it allows us to evolve and work harder to conquer the rough terrain and reach the summit point.

Third, the journey is full of surprises. One of the most exciting things about a journey is that it is full of surprises. We never know what we might encounter or who we might meet along the way. These surprises can be both positive and negative, but they all contribute to the richness and depth of our experience. We might discover a hidden gem that we never would have found, had we just focused on our destination. Not only this, but we might also meet someone who becomes a lifelong friend or mentor. Not just the journey, life itself is full of surprises. If you do not believe in the same, you probably have not yet lived enough to realize it. Very often in life, our plans are changed, and our hopes confounded. Sometimes we are pleasantly surprised. But more often than not, the surprise requires some readjustment and recalibration. We thought we were going down one path, only to be stopped dead in our tracks. Well, we have to turn around, look for a new path, and head there instead.

Lastly, the journey is where memories are made. Well, during the journey, we have the most fun, pleasant laughs, and the most meaningful experiences. If you look back at the last time you went on a trip, you will likely remember the scrumptious food you had eaten, the fun and laughter you had with your friends or family, the new people you met on your journey etc. These things are usually etched forever in the gallery of our hearts. These memories stay with us for a long time, even after we have reached our destination. Memories allow us to live one moment, a thousand times over. It can bring us joy and comfort when we look back on them. In fact, I strongly agree with the statement— *"Sometimes you will never know the value of a moment until it becomes a memory."* Therefore, focus on your journey and create more memories. By focusing on the journey, you will discover that success is not a destination but a continuous process. The failures, the victories, the trials, and the tribulations are all that make lasting impressions more than the ultimate prize. By finding joy in the journey, you celebrate every milestone, no matter how small, and that is where the real victory lies. When you invest in the journey, the destination automatically comes into the picture, not as the end of the road but as the beginning of a new journey.

So, how do we shift our focus from the destination to the journey?

FIRST and foremost, embrace the process. Understand that success, no matter how you define it, is not a straight line. It is a winding path with plenty of twists & turns, followed by uphill struggles and joyful downhill slopes. Remember that this process is perfectly okay. In fact, it is where you evolve as a better human. Do not compare yourself to anyone. Everyone has a different journey and a different story to narrate. There will be several ups and downs, but do not go astray. Keep your focus on what you wish to conquer and take one step at a time. The inevitable truth of life is that things never go as you plan them. Therefore, let things fall into place and embrace randomness.

SECOND, cherish the small victories. Celebrate when you cross a milestone or learn something new. These 'little wins' are signs you are moving ahead in life, however slow it might seem. When you take action and celebrate the tiny victories, you reward yourself for each steppingstone you make to reach your final goals. In fact, when you celebrate small wins, you actually decide to make the mountain you are climbing a little more exciting to handle along your way. When you start giving importance to small victories, you eventually start realizing that you are moving closer to your goal. It further helps you to stay more focused on reaching your destination.

And **FINALLY**, practice mindfulness. Most of the time, our minds wander around in the past or the future rather than in the present. All of us lead extremely busy lives where we are pulled into a million different directions at once. We fail to live in the moment, to *seize the day*. One of the best ways to shift your focus from the destination to the journey is to practice mindfulness. Well, mindfulness is maintaining a crystal-clear awareness of your thoughts, feelings, emotions, bodily sensations, and surroundings. Stay focused on the present moment, take a deep breath, and absorb the moment. Each step on your journey is an experience that shapes you, teaches you, and strengthens you. When we learn to value these moments, the allure of the destination starts to lose its overwhelming obsessive charm.

Our journeys are unique, complex, and beautiful tapestries woven with the threads of experiences, lessons, failures, and triumphs. The destination, the final picture, is undoubtedly important, but it is the journey that lends color, texture, and vibrance to our tapestry. Therefore, savor the journey. When you set out to try something new, never worry about the final destination. Embrace the rollercoaster of experiences. Be passionate about your progress and compassionate about your setbacks. Live in the moments that make up your journey because it is in these moments that you truly find your success, your growth, and ultimately, your happiness. Needless to say, when you thoroughly enjoy the journey, the destination will be beautiful as well.

In case you are still wondering why the journey is more important than the destination, then remember the words of the late chef and author, Anthony Bourdain— *"Travel isn't always pretty. It isn't always comfortable. Sometimes it hurts, it even breaks your heart. But that's okay. The journey changes you; it should change you. It leaves marks on your memory, on your consciousness, on your heart, and on your body. You take something with you. Hopefully, you leave something good behind."*

5
CONCENTRATE ON THE ROAD, NOT THE OBSTACLES

A few years ago in Mumbai, I underwent an intense two-day training program for motorcyclists. A world-renowned motorcycle guru, Brett Tacks, conducted the training program. Brett hailed from the United States of America and has over thirty years of experience in riding and training the best riders in the world. The training program was conducted for off-road riding, preparing one to ride on terrains when no proper road is available. It was spread over two days, and we had multiple obstacle courses. Brett simulated many off-road challenges that riders may usually face. One particular challenge I had to overcome was to ride between two giant craters. It was pretty difficult because there were two deep craters, and I barely had a few inches between them to ride through. I had to keep both my wheels perfectly in that little space in-between, focus, and move ahead without falling into either. Time and again, I lost my focus and failed to accomplish the task.

At that moment, Brett approached me and said, *"You seem to be struggling with this particular one. But you've done so well in much more complex and arduous tasks. Do you know why you are finding this difficult to do? It is because you're focusing on the two big holes in the ground; instead of that narrow little strip of space in the middle, you invariably end up in that ditch."* This phenomenon is called Target fixation— when a rider gets fixed on the biggest obstacle he is trying to avoid. That was when I realized I was trying to avoid falling into those giant craters rather than focusing on riding between them. When I attempted the next time, I came in, and I only looked at that little strip between the craters, and I rode through it without falling into the crater. I could do it again and again, using the same technique. That was when Brett told me that one of the big mistakes many motorcyclists make is- instead of focusing on the road, they focus on the obstacles/challenges. That is where the famous saying among motorcyclists goes, *"Just focus on the road, not the wall."* Because if you focus on the wall, you will end up on the wall. And then, it dawned on me that the lesson I got that day was relevant to motorcycling and life as a whole.

Fast forward to today, I feel that when we actually focus on the problems, we invariably get target fixated. For example, if you are a businessperson and you are focused on not failing—You invariably end up meeting with some kind of failure. But if you are focused on winning, you are more likely to end up on the bright side of things. Albeit unbelievable, it is true that you attract what you focus on. In fact, what you attract is a reflection of what you believe in. Therefore, if you are too engrossed in running away from the possibility of failure instead of focusing on winning, you will face your worst nightmare. The awareness of 'self' motivates one to direct their energy where they want it to be.

Mark Cuban rightly iterates, *"What I've learned in these eleven years is you just gotta stay focused and believe in yourself and trust your own ability and judgment."* My Guru and mentor, the world-renowned personal coach Tony Robbins says, *"Energy flows where the focus goes."* Thus, the question is, what are you focusing on— Consciously or subconsciously, you will always attract what you focus on. To get what you fiercely desire, you require a clear understanding of the goal, which has purpose and meaning behind it. Once your purpose is in place, you can devote your energy to the goal and work towards achieving it.

Let's say you have decided to you have decided to participate in a marathon next year. Now, what will you focus on— improving your overall fitness? Your running speed? Your stamina? Or will you focus on having never run more than three kilometers at a stretch in your life? Will you focus on that nagging knee pain or the fact that most people you know have far more experience in running long distances and have been preparing for a longer period of time than you have? If you focus on the former— your strength, stamina, and fitness, then you give yourself a fighting chance to compete, at least in the half marathon.

However, if you lay more emphasis on the fact that you are in a challenging situation and you have never done something like this before, then you might not even turn up for the event. Therefore, when you are entangled in a crisis next time, observe your thoughts calmly. Ask yourself— Am I focused on things that will help me reach the desired goal? Or am I focused on the obstacles that will prevent me from reaching that goal? In general, this is a spectacular technique if you are trying to do something new. Once you decide to try something new or unconventional, try to evaluate where your focus is at all points and make an effort to move towards things that will help you achieve your goal. Do not panic. Take a deep breath and reduce your focus on the challenges. This is not to imply that one must ignore the challenges and flush them out of sight. However, if you incessantly focus only on the challenges, then you might not be ready to direct yourself towards your desired goal.

Have you ever noticed the impact your thoughts and intentions have on the world around you? As already stated earlier, "energy flows where the focus goes," suggesting that our attention directs the flow of energy and influences our experiences and outcomes. While this concept may seem abstract, numerous examples and research studies support the notion that our intentions have a profound effect on shaping our reality. If you always pick out flaws or pay attention to the negative aspects of life, you invariably cage yourself in the meandering darkness. In simple words, you will be drawn towards negative energy because that is what you are focusing on. Learning how to focus on your energy changes your behavior immediately, giving you the momentum to seize little actions daily that will lead to splendid results. Inculcating this approach in life will help people achieve tasks that once seemed tremendously tricky. It is undoubtedly a powerful tool to help you attain all your life goals. It will help to release all the thirst, desire, and self-belief within you and eliminate distractions, excuses, and self-loathing.

If we look at the 'behind the scenes' life of Thomas Edison, the renowned inventor who invented the incandescent light bulb— we can see this theory in practice. Most people regard Thomas Edison as a genius. To this, Edison always answered, *"Genius is hard work, stick-to-it-iveness, and common sense."* The electric light system was way more than just the incandescent lamp, or "light bulb." A biographer of Edison once said: *"His mother had accomplished that which all truly great teachers do for their pupils. She brought him to the stage of learning things for himself, learning that which most amused and interested him, and she encouraged him to go on in that path. It was the very best thing she could have done for this singular boy."* Edison's relentless focus on creating a long-lasting, practical light source allowed him to channel his energy into countless experiments and eventually find success. Despite facing numerous failures and setbacks, his unwavering intention led him to achieve what many thought was impossible.

Elite athletes often apply visualization techniques to direct their focus and energy toward their desired outcome. They imagine themselves performing flawlessly, effortlessly achieving their goals, and feeling the rush of victory. Visualizing success has been used by athletes throughout the history of humankind. Even ancient Greek wrestlers were known to use visualization techniques to prepare themselves mentally before participating in a competition. Research in sports psychology has shown that this form of mental rehearsal can enhance performance, increase motivation, and boost overall confidence. By picturing yourself achieving success in advance, you can reduce any anxiety or imposter syndrome about your ability to thrive in life. As a professional tennis player, Serena Williams often faced difficult opponents and long matches that could be mentally exhausting. She used visualization to calm her nerves before a match, which allowed her to stay focused while playing. The late Kobe Bryant too, used the visualization technique to stay motivated and attain game-winning shots. By actively focusing their energy on success, athletes attract opportunities, overcome obstacles, and ultimately propel themselves toward greatness.

The concept of energy flows where the focus goes also finds resonance in the realm of interpersonal relationships. The emotions we encounter in our regular lives are intimately tied to our overall quality of life. It indicates that the more we feel excitement, the more we connect with having a fulfilled existence. And the more we doubt ourselves and contemplate the possibility of a situation getting worse, it actually turns out to be true. A part of being human means facing the brutalities of life. After all, we live in binary— There is no light without darkness, no mirth without grief. However, enduring negative energy daily bears no fruit. Tell me, have you ever noticed how a negative mindset can attract negative experiences? When we constantly dwell on what is wrong or expend our energy on negative thoughts, we inadvertently invite more negativity into our lives. Relationships deteriorate, opportunities dwindle, and our overall well-being suffers. Conversely, when we shift our focus to gratitude, positivity, and love, we often see a transformation in our interactions and circumstances. By directing our energy towards fostering healthy connections and embracing a positive mindset, we create a ripple effect that attracts more positivity and happiness into our lives.

Beyond anecdotal evidence, scientific research supports the notion that energy follows focus. The human mind and water are two parallel yet separate derivatives of nature. Dr. Masaru Emoto, a Japanese businessperson, author, and scientist, claimed that human consciousness could affect the molecular structure of water. In his study, he explored the effects of intention and consciousness on water molecules. In his experiment, Dr. Emoto exposed water samples to both positive and negative thoughts, emotions, and intentions. He froze the samples and examined the resulting ice crystals under a microscope. Surprisingly, the water exposed to positive intentions displayed beautifully formed crystals, resembling intricate snowflakes. Conversely, the water exposed to negative intentions exhibited chaotic and distorted crystalline structures. This groundbreaking study provided visual evidence that our thoughts and intentions can influence the molecular structure of water, highlighting the potential impact on our physical environment. Dr. Emoto says, *"Words are the vibrations of nature. Therefore, beautiful words create beautiful nature. Ugly words create ugly nature. This is the root of the universe."*

Additionally, research in the field of quantum physics supports the idea that our thoughts and intentions influence the flow of energy. Whatever you imagine, exists in the form of energy. If you imagine a luxurious holiday, then that holiday already exists, but in an energy wave form. It is our thoughts and intentions that will turn this energy waveform into our experience. Quantum physicists have discovered that at a subatomic level, particles can exhibit both wave-like and particle-like properties. The famous double-slit experiment demonstrates that the act of observation affects the behavior of particles. When observed, particles behave as particles, but when unobserved, they act as waves that can exist in multiple places simultaneously. An individual's thoughts can manipulate and influence subatomic particles. Therefore, you can alter what is around you simply by using your thoughts. This experiment hints at a fundamental truth— our consciousness and intention shape the very fabric of reality. Wallace Wattles, the author of *The Science of Getting Rich*, said, *"There is a thinking stuff from which all the things are made and which, in its actual state, permeates, penetrates, and fills the interspaces of the universe."*

So, how do we develop the ability to focus on the positive aspects rather than on the negative ones?

The very **FIRST** thing to do is embrace optimism. It instills a belief in our ability to create positive change and contributes to a healthy and motivated state of mind. When we marinate our minds with healthy and positive thoughts, we thrive in our personal and professional lives. However, when we fail to nourish them, we deprive ourselves from being happy and tend to constantly put ourselves down. For example, if you fear failing a test, will it do you any good? Does the constant thought of "What if I'm not able to pass this?" help in any way? Being optimistic will benefit both your mental and physical health. It helps lower stress, improve immunity, and build resilience. If you are optimistic, things can work out in some way or the other. Focusing more on the positive aspects will help individuals in keeping a distance from the negative thoughts.

The **SECOND** thing to keep in mind is having solution-oriented thinking. Focusing on solutions rather than obstacles enables us to break free from limiting beliefs and turn obstacles into steppingstones. A growth mindset enables an individual to stay on track to explore new opportunities. Being solution-oriented implies that you refuse to sleep until you find the answer to your problems. One must discipline themselves to be hungry and search for the answers. Overcoming obstacles requires a paradigm shift. The choice is yours— To either let the problem devour you or you choose to give your sweat and blood to fight against the odds facing you. Every problem has a hidden solution. You need to be patient and creative enough to find it. Solution-oriented people do not just solve problems. They identify the source of an issue and provide the right way of doing things. Being solution-oriented allows you to think critically. It helps you evaluate, analyze, and have clarity to solve many issues.

FINALLY, develop mindfulness and visualization skills. These are powerful tools that will help in channelizing our energy towards the desired outcomes. Practicing mindfulness helps in increasing the efficiency of brain pathways that process information. In other words, it boosts your attention and helps you gain a clear perspective. By focusing on the present moment and cultivating mindful awareness, you can actually improve your brain's ability to direct your attention and accurately perceive the world through a clean lens. Whenever you feel worried, put all of your focus on your breath. I believe it is a portal into the present moment and definitely the best cure for stress. The secret power of visualization can help attain success. The process of imagining yourself accomplishing what you want to achieve is actually winning half the battle. If you look at Jim Carrey— While grappling with looking for work, he had written himself a post-dated $10 million cheque, due a couple of years later. By the year 1995, right before the cheque would have expired—Carrey got his big break as an actor and was offered $10 million to star in *Dumb and Dumber*. Visualization is not magic, nor is it similar to a "quick way to get rich" scheme. Instead, it is an additional tool to propel towards realizing and living the desired dreams.

Thus, from this chapter, we have learned that it is vital to focus on the road and not the obstacles. Businessperson and author Ben Horowitz noted, "When someone learns to drive a race car, one of the first lessons taught is that when you are going around a curve at 200 mph, do not focus on the wall; focus on the road. If you focus on the wall, you will drive right into it. If you focus on the road, you follow the road. Running a company is like that." Being engrossed over "what ifs" and fear of failure ultimately leads to nothing. In the end, your energy will be directed toward the flow of your focus. By embracing optimism, having a solution-oriented mind, and developing mindfulness and visualization skills, one can focus on the positive aspects of life rather than driving towards negative energy. If you still find yourself stumbling more upon the wall, the fear of failure, and the negative aspects, remember the words of Tony Robbins — *"Stop being afraid of what could go wrong, and start being excited of what could go right."*

6
AVOID SHORTCUTS

"Avoid shortcuts, for they may cut your life short." I found this inscribed in a milestone while traveling to Ladakh. You may find several other quotes like these while traveling in the mountains. The B.R.O (Border Road Organization) has had this tradition of putting out statutory warnings in a light-hearted way, which you will come across while traveling on treacherous roads in the mountains for many years now. Some of these 'pieces of advice' might not be grammatically correct, but they rhyme and are memorable.

In 2021, as per the Road and Service Transport Ministry of India statistics, 55% of accidents were caused by speeding, and another 25% approximately were caused by dangerous, reckless, and wrong overtaking. According to the National Crime Records Bureau, in 2021, 1,50,000 people died on Indian roads. This has consistently increased as the vehicular population and the general population rise year on year. So, that's about 370 people dying every day because they are trying to reach their destination faster than they were initially supposed to. That is a startling number of people who lost their lives because they were impatient while they were on the road and wanted to get ahead quickly for no apparent reason. And that is precisely the point I am trying to make about shortcuts.

Shortcuts are about trying to find a more accessible, quicker, faster path to reach your destination than they were initially supposed to do. People want to achieve things quickly – get to places faster, grow their start-ups faster, achieve personal milestones earlier, become rich speedily, and so on. And to help people achieve these goals there are tens of thousands of self-help books. However, much like in motorcycling, shortcuts are absolutely dangerous in life, too. The human brain naturally tends to cut corners, arising out of an intrinsic need to conserve energy and work more efficiently. Unfortunately, this part of the brain operates from a slightly irrational side and cannot always recognize the risk associated with it. Therefore, it is not your primordial brain functioning here but that little-developed brain whose fight or flight assessing faculty is not entirely at play. When the brain looks at conserving energy faster, it pushes us towards making impulsive, not so well thought through decisions. At that moment, it may look very apt, but in retrospect, you may have avoided making that call had you paused. If I were to watch a video compilation (if it was available) of all my motorcycling mishaps, I would curse myself for the stupid decisions I took just before the crash, but in real life, it all felt like the correct choice. Therefore, human beings naturally tend to take shortcuts, thereby risking things, but the problem is that they often fall for those tempting shortcut decisions. It is not just the risk for yourself; it is the risk for others as well. Most of these road accidents have fatalities beyond just the person driving or who made the decision. Sadly, a large number of people have paid with their lives for someone else's wrong decision or a shortcut temptation.

Shortcuts are tempting, but there is more to lose than gain if you fall for it. In a world driven by instant gratification and quick fixes, it is easy to be drawn to take shortcuts. Do you think Mark Zuckerberg took just one day to discover Facebook? Do you feel Shah Rukh Khan earned the title "King Khan of Bollywood" by slaying in just one movie? Or do you think "The Beatles" earned their fame overnight? Obviously not, right? It takes years of constant hard work, confidence, dedication, a never-giving-up attitude, and avoiding the shortcuts to success to reach where they are today. Success is time-consuming and a long journey to embark on. Since people, in general, are very impatient, a lot of them are on the lookout for shortcuts. However, one must remember that true success and fulfilment come from putting in the necessary effort and taking the longer, more arduous path. You cannot suddenly expect to emerge more vigorous when you avoid hardships. Nobody has ever said they are thankful for the shortcuts because those are always momentary. I agree that shortcuts may offer immediate benefits, but they often lead to more harm than good in the long run.

Let us try to explore this notion and provide examples and key points as to why one shouldn't take shortcuts in life. Firstly, taking shortcuts undermines personal growth and development. Most people need to realize that taking shortcuts hinders their room for learning. While shortcuts may result in quick conclusions, they often disrupt the vital learning process, resilience-building, and character development. The journey toward success is not solely about making tangible accomplishments but also about building character, resilience, and knowledge. When we take shortcuts, we bypass the valuable lessons that challenges and failures impart to us. Avoiding shortcuts in life is a valuable life lesson that nurtures holistic growth and enduring fulfillment in life. These hardships shape us, pushing us out of our comfort zones and teaching us invaluable skills that will serve us later in life. By failing to embrace the process, we deny ourselves the opportunity to grow into the best versions of ourselves.

For instance, let us consider a student who is preparing to crack the IIT entrance exam, considered one of toughest ones. Instead of investing time and effort into studying thoroughly, he/she opts for shortcuts like mugging the answers or even cheating. While these tactics may yield temporary success, such as passing the exam, they fail to equip the student with the knowledge and skills they need to succeed in the long term. In the end, the lack of a solid foundation will have repercussions, impeding their progress in future endeavors. Similarly, in the professional field, if your boss asks you to create a presentation and you refrain from doing any proper research and just cut paste some information from the internet because it was the easier thing to do, you are likely to create an average presentation. More often than not short cuts often compromise the quality of the final outcome.

If you aim to achieve something stupendous- be it in a business, your professional life, or anything in general; it is vital not to take the easy way out because the outcome will not be satisfying. It is perfectly fine to dig out ways that are more creative and efficient but keep the end results intact. In reality, success stories do not churn overnight. They require years of dedication, hard work, and commitment to get to that point. Whether it be in professional pursuits, personal relationships, or creative endeavors, rushing through the process can result in subpar results. True excellence requires meticulous attention to detail and a commitment to doing things the right way, not the easiest way. The author Thomas Stark says, *"There are no shortcuts. The lazy will accomplish nothing in life. The human path of least resistance is the path to total failure and oblivion. You must always walk the hard path. The fewer the people on the path, the greater the glory. A genius is alone on his path."* Momentarily, you might have the relief of being able to finish the assigned work, but later it will affect your career curve. Therefore, by avoiding shortcuts and committing to deep learning, this student/employee can acquire knowledge that will remain valuable long after the exam/project is over.

Imagine an aspiring chef who decides to take shortcuts in the kitchen. Do you think they will be able to acquire all the skills to ace their job? Instead of dedicating time to learning and mastering cooking techniques, they rely on pre-packaged, ready-to-cook meals. While this may save time, it significantly diminishes the quality and creativity of their culinary creations. By taking the longer route of honing their culinary skills and experimenting with different flavors and techniques, they can develop their unique style and create extraordinary dishes that stand out among the rest. In a similar fashion, if a Ph.D. student decides not to research hundreds of journals and write their thesis hastily, and submit a half-baked concept, do you think their paper will hold any value? Taking the shorter route may be easy but it will fetch zero results eventually. After all, nothing good has ever come out of hurry and frustration, only misery.

In addition to hindering personal growth and compromising quality, shortcuts also pose risks to one's integrity and reputation. The author Daniel H. Pink validates this point in his quote— *"The problem with making an extrinsic reward the only destination that matters is that some people will choose the quickest route there, even if it means taking the low road. Indeed, most of the scandals and misbehavior that have seemed endemic to modern life involve shortcuts."* Taking dishonest shortcuts can tarnish one's credibility and erode trust, both of which are essential in personal and professional relationships. In order to build a solid foundation of trust, it is crucial to demonstrate integrity and a commitment to doing things ethically and honestly.

For instance, an employee who resorts to unethical practices to gain a promotion may succeed temporarily. However, their actions will eventually come to light, leading to severe consequences such as termination or damaged relationships with colleagues. Likewise, if a student decides to cheat in an exam and gets caught, their reputation will be damaged forever. Not just their reputation, they might be abstained from taking any more examinations and can even be expelled. In contrast, an employee or student who chooses not to take shortcuts and instead focuses on building their skills, studying hard, contributing meaningfully, and demonstrating integrity will be recognized for their genuine efforts and ethical conduct. Ultimately, their reputation will be untarnished and better positioned for long-term success and advancement.

Hence, while shortcuts may appear attractive and alluring, the long-term drawbacks outweigh the initial benefits. By succumbing to the temptation of quick fixes, one risks hindering personal growth, compromising the quality of their work, and damaging their integrity and reputation. Instead, it is important to embrace the journey, challenge oneself, and commit to doing things the right way. Only through perseverance and hard work can we achieve true success and find fulfilment. So, resist the allure of shortcuts and embark on the path less traveled, for richness and reward await those who choose the road less hurried.

So, how can we avoid falling into the shortcut thinking trap?

FIRST, define your long-term goals: Make a clear list of your long-term aspirations and what success means to you. This clarity will help you direct your goals towards the desired direction. Knowing where you want to go can help you stay focused and resist the temptation of shortcuts that may distract you from your ultimate objectives. For instance, if you aim to be an entrepreneur, you must thoroughly research and be aware of your resources. Take guidance from seniors or people who have already excelled in this field. Be clear about where you should put in and how much effort. In this way, you can save up a lot of time and energy to make concrete decisions.

SECOND, visualize the bigger picture. Take a step back and visualize the long-term impact of your actions. As human beings, it is natural to want instant success but always keep in mind that overnight success is usually short-term. You have to understand that shortcuts may provide temporary satisfaction or quick wins but may hinder your progress toward larger, more fulfilling goals in the long run. Always keep the bigger picture in mind. Do not get disheartened by a few barriers. After all, as the old adage says, *"Failures are the steppingstones to success."* All your hard work and efforts will be worth it. If you have honest intentions and give genuine efforts, you will attain whatever you want to.

THIRD, embrace delayed gratification: You must understand that significant achievements often require time, effort, and perseverance. After all, Rome was not built in one day. You cannot achieve wonders on a particular day. It always takes years of dedication and commitment to reach the final destination. Therefore, expect a delay in your long-term success. You have to accept the fact that you cannot turn everything according to your desires overnight. Once you do this, the process gets easier. In fact, embrace the whole journey.

Learn to cultivate the mindset of delayed gratification, focusing on the joy and fulfilment that comes from working diligently towards long-term success instead of seeking instant gratification from shortcuts.

FOURTH, make a commitment to consistency: You have to commit yourself to consistent effort and discipline. As already mentioned, multiple times, unless you get into the habit of doing something consistently, you will not be able to ace it. "Persevere to the end" should always be your motto. Even if you get tired of doing the same thing every day, keep doing it. Keep giving efforts where it is necessary. Follow a routine and be dedicated to your goals and aspirations. Instead of seeking shortcuts, prioritize creating positive habits that align with your long-term goals. You must remember that consistent small steps in the right direction can lead to significant long-term success.

To move further, one should seek inspiration and guidance: It is not shameful if you have to seek help from anyone. In fact, sometimes you get the best advice from strangers than your own friends and well-wishers. Be a good communicator and surround yourself with individuals who inspire and motivate you. Make sure you are always surrounded by the right kind of energy and that you feel heavily motivated to fulfill your dreams. Seek mentors or role models who have achieved long-term success and learn from their journeys. The first thing you will learn from them is that there are no shortcuts to success. In fact, their experiences can reinforce the importance of prioritizing long-term fulfillment over short-term shortcuts.

The next step is to avoid comparison: It is human nature to often compare yourself with other individuals. Unfortunately, most of us have been facing this since our childhood. It is very common nowadays especially due to constant validation and hullabaloo in social media. But no matter what, try to resist the urge to compare your progress or success to others, especially when it comes to shortcuts they may have taken. Always remember that your journey is different from others. You may not have the same privileges as someone else. Therefore, they might attain success way before you. But do not get disheartened or get driven by imposter syndrome. Remember that everyone's journey is unique, and focusing on your path will enhance your chances of long-term success.

FINALLY, reflect on personal values and purpose: You must regularly remind yourself of your core values and personal purpose. Never forget your values and the purpose of having your personalized goals. You must align your actions and decisions with these guiding principles. They will help you make choices that prioritize long-term success and authentic fulfilment rather than taking shortcuts that compromise your values. Always be honest with yourself and keep believing in yourself. The journey is never going to be easy. But you have to keep going.

In this fast-paced world, anyone will likely choose a shortcut rather than struggle for years. But whenever you feel tempted to give up on your goals, remember this quote: *"One thing was certain: life was a maze. There was nothing straightforward. Everything that pretended to be straight somehow ended in unexpected twists and turns, only to leave you full of wonder at how you possibly made it through to the end. You couldn't just pack a pair of hedge trimmers to take a shortcut and hoodwink fate. No, you had to walk the path of life given to you with all its detours. The goal wasn't to avoid getting lost sometimes—in fact, that was most unlikely given that you were in a maze. The trick was simply to keep walking. To enjoy the process of getting lost and finding yourself again, different, and more grown-up than when you had left. One step after another, that was all that it took. One step after another, so simple and so utterly enough."*

7
KNOW YOUR LIMITS

"How few there are who have courage enough to own their faults or resolution enough to mend them."
–Benjamin Franklin

While I agree that people should never let any limitations restrict them from moving further in life, it is vital to know your weakness. Being aware of your drawbacks helps you to understand yourself better. Jumping into the shortcut of victory without being cautious of your whereabouts can lead to a fall in the future. Even the greatest champions were aware of their limitations. Some of them understood the conditions that worked for them and those that did not. The seven-time world Champion of Formula One racing, Michael Schumacher, was never the fastest driver on the grid, even when he was winning races every weekend. He was the most efficient racer. Therefore, he never pushed to set lap records, but over the forty laps of a race, he successfully developed a consistent pace, conserved his tires, and made his opponents wear out their tires and resolved to beat him. He won seven world championships during his illustrious racing career not just because he knew his opponent's limitations but, most importantly, his own limitations. Michael had every track in F1 in his mental computer, and he drove from his memory when visibility was an issue, making him the 'rain master'. Thus, knowing your limits and being aware of others can help you achieve your goals in life.

A lot of motorcycle enthusiasts often make silly mistakes and end up with a crash when riding in a group. However, they make very few mistakes when they ride alone. This usually happens because they are trying to emulate other riders in the group who may have superior skills like taking a fast corner, thereby pushing themselves beyond their limits. If they rode within their limits, they certainly would have made fewer mistakes and had lesser crashes. The idea of surpassing everyone has often been ingrained in us, and we forget that if we cross our limitations, there will be severe consequences. People fail to realize that going with the masses and not being cautious of their surroundings often leads to their downfall. I see this trend in many aspects of life— be it career, business, parenting etc. People push themselves beyond their limits because of their peer group. Instead, if they focused solely on their own skills and not get influenced by others, they are likely to create wonders. If you stay within your limits, then you are safe more often than not. Knowing when to take a leap of faith and when to guard yourself are two different things. A wise person is always somebody who knows the difference between the two. A lot of us try new things without doing proper research. When you explore new areas of interest, thoroughly understanding the challenges and your limitations is always better before you take the leap.

So, how do you know what your limits are? By falling? Or by not trying? I believe that you will know your limits by understanding who you truly are and what matters to you the most. So, sit down and ask yourself— What do you want in life? What are your dreams and aspirations? Why do you want it? What are you willing to sacrifice to achieve your dreams and goals, and why? What is the price you are willing to pay? What are you unwilling to give up to achieve your dreams and goals? You need clarity to answer these questions. This self-reflection will help you understand yourself better. Once you have the answers, you will know your drawbacks or limits. The moment you become clear about your inner desires and what you want, it will be easier for you to pave your road map. Well, the very first thing to keep in mind is do not compare yourself with others. Do not try to fit in with others and follow in their footsteps. Do not try to become somebody you are not. What I mean by this is— Do not jump into a well just because everyone is doing it. Do not buy the latest electronic gadgets just because someone else is doing it, too. Do not start a business or quit your current job just because your peers are doing it. Do not buy a superbike or a house just because you saw your neighbor doing the same. Ask yourself— Is it a part of your dreams and goals? Will this help or benefit you in any way? What are you willing to sacrifice for it? What is your risk appetite?

In order to test your limits, you need to truly know yourself. You need to know your flaws. You need to know where you stand in life. Everyone has their flaws. Nobody is perfect. In fact, most of the time it is these flaws that tip us over while we are in the pursuit of our passions. In fact, as Marilyn Monroe says, "Imperfection is beauty, madness is genius, and it's better to be absolutely ridiculous than absolutely boring." Each one of us is wired with a distinctive set of skills, talents, and inclinations. Our strengths are the sails that propel us forward, but our limitations anchor us, providing stability amidst the tumultuous waves of enterprise. Recognizing our flaws instills wisdom that is instrumental in charting our individual paths and forging a collective journey marked by integrity, resilience, and ingenuity. But how do we embark upon this journey of self-discovery? It begins with introspection followed by diving deep into the ocean of our psyche, acknowledging the expanse of our strengths, and the boundaries marked by our limitations. It is a pursuit of self-awareness, where we juxtapose our inner world against external realities, drawing profound and transformative insights.

Here are my flaws that I unearthed while on a journey inward. Truth to be told, this list has been collected over many inward journeys over many years.

My inability to say "NO" to people in my circle has often led to my downfall. I have often held myself back from saying "NO" because I worry about hurting the other person's feelings. My usual behavior to see how I can make it happen is to think through the pitfalls of every proposal that is in front of me, especially coming from my close circles. I am still in the process of forming my own boundaries, but ever since I figured out my flaws, things became a little easier.

My lack of attention to detail is a flaw that I am still working on. I often get excited by the "bigger picture" and do not labor over-crossing the "t's" and dotting the "i's." In doing this, I find it difficult to focus more on the details. Sometimes, I fail to read between the lines and get a clear vision. Therefore, I need to overcome this flaw. To be honest, I also have a threshold level of boredom too. I get bored easily if something does not interest me. I lose focus on a task if it is mundane and lacks newness. I fail to understand that not everything is going to always be interesting. I have been working hard to change this for a while now.

Sometimes I feel I am not pushy enough. I barely ever ask anyone for the same thing more than twice. I feel I will come off as a nagging person if I keep checking up. I give up if the answer is negative in the first two attempts. Sometimes persuasion is important, but I fail to do so. I talk more than I listen. This is an inherent flaw in me. I fail to keep up with reading the room. I often keep talking so much that I overlook that the other person also has something to say. Twenty-seven years in the business of persuasion made me go off the block faster than others in meetings or discussions. I believe I need to curb this and listen to others more.

I also believe that mild to low instances of procrastination have embraced me, especially on matters of self. As a professional, I was always proactive and diligent in the tasks I had to complete, but that diligence never shone through in my personal life. My inability to drive a hard bargain has often put me in uncomfortable situations. I could never put the 'shylock' mode on any negotiation. I fail at it miserably. My inherent sense of fairness made me leave a lot of money on the table. However, I do not regret any of those instances anytime I re-think about it.

So, can you put down a list of your 'best' flaws that you have discovered about yourself?

It is easier said than done and will take much longer than you expect to arrive at a list which you can be comfortable with. But the process of self-discovery is therapeutic and liberating at the same time. When we confront our flaws, we unlock the power of adaptation. We learn to pivot, evolve, and transform our strategies, aligning them with the ever-changing business landscapes. Every limitation then transforms into a steppingstone; each challenge is a catalyst propelling us toward uncharted territories marked by innovation, creativity, and excellence.

The acknowledgment of our flaws fosters a culture of collaboration and inclusivity. In the journey of life, success is not a solitary pursuit. It is a collective journey where the amalgamation of diverse talents, skills, and perspectives forge a pathway marked by innovation and sustainability. Our limitations are the bridges that connect us to others, fostering dynamic and regenerative synergies.

Knowing our limits is not a destination. It is a journey – an ongoing process of self-discovery, learning, and evolution. Every day presents a new opportunity to confront our boundaries, to push against the confines, and to emerge not just as leaders but as visionaries who are not confined by the limits but are defined by their ability to transcend them. But knowing your limitations makes you a fantastic rider who can maximize your joy of riding (and living) while on your chosen path.

8
THE FALL IS NOT THE END

"The splendid thing about falling apart silently is that you can start over as many times as you like."

–Anonymous

Falls are bound to happen, but what you do after the fall is what really matters. The year was 1994 when I came to Bombay (Now Mumbai) to pursue my higher education and career. I was very excited to explore the various corners of this amazing city and I used my spare time to map the popular and not so popular parts of the city. Though Mumbai has a fantastic public transport system, I somehow felt the handicap of not having personal transport, which at best could only be a two-wheeler given my life stage. Truth be told, I was salivating on a particular brand of motorcycle with a Czech heritage called Yezdi. Two Parsi gentlemen bought the rights to the Czech brand called Jawa and Indianized the name to Yezdi in 1960. Since then, it has become a cult brand in India, and the best-maintained Yezdis are with Parsi owners. Parsis and Yezdis were a match made in heaven, and the bikes looked brand new even if they were a decade old. With much difficulty (try convincing a Parsi to part with his motorcycle), I bought a Parsi-owned Yezdi Road King. I had the best time of my life with this prized possession of mine flying up and down the streets of Bombay for years. Until one eventful night, when I met with a severe accident. That accident was so drastic and dramatic that many people feared for my life. But somehow, I survived it albeit with some serious injuries, which had me lying on my back and staring at the ceiling for a long time. Everyone I knew told me to refrain from riding motorcycles ever again and give up on this "madness." At that time, Bombay was not a city of two-wheelers like today. Most people use public transport such as local trains, buses, and occasionally taxis. My colleagues and a few friends felt I was trying to be a little obsessive about something you can do without, especially in a city like Bombay.

After taking the long road to recovery, I first convinced my dad to lend me some money to buy another motorcycle. Logic said no more motorcycles, but heart said otherwise. I knew that if I gave up riding then I would never return to it ever. The accident was fresh in my memory. I somehow felt very deeply about riding motorcycles, and I wanted to continue it for as long as I was able to. That was a defining moment in my life, whether I walked away from something I truly cared about or garnered all the courage to get back on a motorcycle and ride again. Thankfully, I listened to my heart and repurchased a motorcycle.

Most of us who ride motorcycles have stories of some crashes or the other. It is the nature of the game. But many people who get themselves a motorcycle late in life realize this the hard way. After their first hard crash, they literally reach a crossroad – to keep or sell. The advice, and concerns of family and friends around them also play a very important role in this. Above anything, their confidence takes a big beating, and soon, the motorcycle will be put on an auction site and sold. The dream comes to a grinding halt. Much like that, I have seen people give up on their life dreams, whether it is about doing something on their own or pursuing something that they never pursued- a new venture, a pet project, or even a simple thing such as a weekend gig. They go about initially with much passion and put in a lot of effort to pursue it with all the enthusiasm they can muster. But in motorcycling, they will also meet with a significant failure or major roadblock somewhere down the line. Their enthusiasm will dwindle, and doubts will start creeping in because they believe that the first crash is a sign, or worse, the end of the road. Everyone who ever rode a motorcycle has fallen at least once.

Similarly, anyone who tried to build something new has faced a challenge. Even the world's best riders would have spent a few days in the hospital and had broken bones. The world's best entrepreneurs would have had many stories of failures or near bankruptcies, but that never deterred them from pursuing their dreams and finally making a success out of their endeavors.

Even the Iron Man was a failure in life initially. Well, not Ironman, the Marvel hero, but Robert Downey Jr., who played Ironman, is an amazing case study about resurrecting from his colossal failures. Robert Downey Jr. was born in New York. And his story is indeed one of the greatest comeback stories, not just of Hollywood, but of an entire world of entertainment. Robert did have a family background in the entertainment industry. His father and mother were both actors but not very recognized ones. At a young age, he began acting and gained recognition in the 80s and 90s for some outstanding performances in various films. He quickly became one of his generation's most promising and talented actors and a future hero to be counted on. However, it was not all smooth sailing thereon because the initial success had a different impact on Robert Downey Jr's life. He became addicted to drugs and alcohol, which began to affect his personal life. And, of course, his substance abuse problem was so intense that it led to multiple run-ins with authorities, like failing drug tests and probation violations. He visited rehabilitation centers numerous times, but it was not successful. He was in and out of them regularly.

During this dark phase of his life, his career ultimately suffered. All the studios and production companies who wanted him initially withdrew their contract in quick succession. They completely deserted him because he was a mess, which they never wanted to be a part of. While the world gave up on him, his wife took it upon herself to turn his life around. In 2003, he entered a court-ordered rehab program again and began his journey toward recovery and reform. His determination, along with the support of his partner, finally helped him to kick the habit. Hollywood also gave him a second chance, and he landed the critically acclaimed film. *Kiss Kiss Bang Bang* in 2005. His performance in that movie caught the eye of the makers of the Marvel Cinematic Universe superhero genre. They took the chance on Robert and cast him as the Marvel superhero– Tony Stark, aka Iron Man. The release of *Avengers* marked the turnaround of Robert Downey Jr's career and life. Not only the movie but also the entire series became worldwide blockbusters. He eventually became the highest-earning Hollywood hero of all time, along with becoming a cult figure with a global fan following. Robert

Downey Jr went on to act in the Sherlock Holmes franchise, which won him the Golden Globe nomination in the Best Actor category. Imagine if Robert and his partner were to give up after the repeated falls in his life earlier, the world wouldn't have known a star called Robert Downey Jr.

If you take a look at the most inspirational entrepreneurs, athletes, and actors throughout history, they share a common belief of not accepting failure. Instead, they rose like a phoenix each time they fell and did not entertain the notion of failure as bad. Thomas Edison perfectly captures this notion in his famous quote— *"I have not failed. I've just found 10,000 ways that won't work."* You may think— Why do so many individuals abandon their dreams after one failed attempt rather than persist in the face of adversity? This perplexing phenomenon opens a window into the complexities of human psychology, societal pressures, and the harsh realities of our modern world. Most people fail to realize that good things take time, and sometimes, even if it may feel overwhelming to keep going, the wait is worth it. Be it the fear of failure, lack of motivation, or zero self-confidence, people find it challenging to stay motivated and determined when obstacles arise. For most people it is easy to try once, fail, and then lament, "I already tried, and I didn't win so let me give up." Even though most of you may not agree with me, I believe that giving up permits you a reason to sit and be angry at the world instead of looking out for your own well-being. "Most people overestimate what they can achieve in a couple of years and underestimate what they can achieve in a decade" says Tony Robbins and I cannot agree with him more.

One of the key factors contributing to the abandonment of dreams after a single setback is the innate fear of failure. Most of the time, the thought of failure itself is greater than the fear of the unknown. The anxiety of not measuring up to one's own expectations and the fear of judgment from others can be paralyzing. In a society that often celebrates only the end result and overlooks the struggle behind success, failure can feel like an indelible stain on one's identity. Failure can be very intimidating and complex to deal with. The emotional consequences of failing at something can be terrifying. In fact, failure is often seen as a reflection of our abilities and self-worth. Therefore, most people find it convenient to give up on what they worked hard on and try something new again. However, the attitude of quitting after one failed attempt eventually leads to a lot of regret. Not only the fear of failure, but unrealistic expectations can also be an enormous source of frustration, disappointment, and stress. Thus, it is vital to have realistic goals and a proper pattern to reach the desired destination.

I have witnessed countless instances where individuals let go of their aspirations due to the fear of failure, retreating to what they perceive as safer grounds rather than risking further disappointment. Moreover, the instant gratification culture of our times exacerbates the problem. We have grown accustomed to quick results, whether in the form of social media validation or instant success stories. Truth to be told, a lot of people lack patience— the patience to strive harder, the patience to try something new even if the planned objective does not work out, the patience to deal with obstacles and wait for results. The concept of perseverance, of toiling away for an extended period with no immediate rewards, seems alien to many. The reality is that achieving one's dreams often involves an arduous journey littered with failures that pave the way for eventual success. The idea of putting in prolonged effort without seeing quick progress can be a bitter pill to swallow, leading individuals to abandon their dreams prematurely. However, I firmly believe that you have to fail if you wish to succeed. The road map to success is always nonlinear. One has to try and try time and again and rise above everything to reach their goal.

Not only failure, but even societal pressures also lead to people giving up on their dreams. From an early age, we are programmed to conform to established norms and benchmarks of success. Parents, peers, and even cultural narratives can instill rigid definitions of achievement, leaving little room for deviation. All of us have a desire to be accepted and validated by others. A lot of people internalize external validation so much that they feel their worth is determined by how other people perceive us. In the face of societal expectations, the fear of disappointing loved ones can become a formidable barrier to persisting in the pursuit of one's dreams. Several teenagers give up on their dream careers and passions just to please their parents. This has been an emerging issue in our world. In fact, this is precisely the reason why several students give up quickly because they do not have goals mapped for themselves, but for their parents. Similarly, several grown-ups fear doing what they love because there is an underlying fear of disappointing their families. This pressure to conform can easily lead to the forfeiture of personal aspirations for the sake of meeting external standards.

In our digital age, comparisons have become more relentless than ever. Social media offers an endless scroll of others' achievements, curated to perfection. This constant exposure to seemingly unattainable success stories can fuel feelings of inadequacy and discourage individuals from persisting after a single setback. The ease with which we can glimpse into the lives of others has unwittingly become a double-edged sword, providing inspiration but also triggering self-doubt. As we navigate the complex labyrinth of why people abandon their dreams after a solitary failure, it's crucial to acknowledge that the journey of realizing one's aspirations is rarely linear. In fact, setbacks and failures are integral to growth and success. As a society, we must foster an environment that celebrates resilience, emphasizes the importance of learning from failure, and offers support to those who stumble. So, what strategies can one use to bounce back from these setbacks while chasing our dreams? Certainly, bouncing back from setbacks while pursuing your dreams and maintaining resilience is a crucial skill.

Here are some strategies drawn from behavioral science and self-help principles that can help you stay motivated and not give up too soon:

The **FIRST** thing is to have a resilience mindset. Develop a resilient mindset by understanding that setbacks are a natural part of any journey. Do not see setbacks or hurdles as a reason to quit. No matter what you do in life, there will always be a struggle. Do not give up easily. Keep a check on the bigger picture. View the hurdles as opportunities for growth and learning rather than failures. Embrace challenges as steppingstones toward your ultimate goal.

The **SECOND** factor is to set realistic expectations. While having big dreams is important, setting unrealistic expectations can lead to disappointment. Break down your goals into smaller, achievable milestones. Refrain from dwelling into unrealistic goals with no roadmap. Have a clear understanding of what you want. Celebrate each accomplishment along the way to keep yourself motivated. Embrace the journey and keep track of your accomplishments.

The **THIRD** thing to keep in mind is to have positive self-talk. One of the major things that people lack is positivity, especially about themselves. Do not give into self-loathing. There will always be several people out there to speak ill of you. Do not waste your time doing it. Once you practice positive self-talk and affirmations, you will be able to move further in life. Replace negative thoughts with constructive and motivating statements. This can help you maintain a positive outlook, even in the face of setbacks.

The **FOURTH** factor that helps is the power of adaptability. Nothing is constant in life. Not everything will work out the way you plan them. Everything you decide to do is likely to have certain ups and downs. It is the law of the universe. Make sure you are willing to adapt your strategies and approaches when faced with setbacks. Embrace the uncomfortable, the fear of the unknown, and be dynamic. Have a growth mindset. Flexibility allows you to find alternative paths and solutions to reach your goals.

The **FIFTH** point is to learn from failure. No man has been born who has not failed at something. You cannot rise with your head held high unless you fall into the ashes. Instead of dwelling on failure, analyze what went wrong and what you can learn from the experience. Do not accept a one-time or more than that failure as a final mark to your journey. Every setback contains valuable lessons that can contribute to your personal and professional growth.

The **NEXT** important thing is to build a support system. As much as you should believe in yourself, make sure you have people in your life who add positivity too. Surround yourself with supportive individuals who believe in your dreams. Therefore, it is vital to choose the right kind of energy. Share your setbacks with them and allow them to provide encouragement and advice. Sometimes, an outsider's perspective can offer valuable insights. Analyze their feedback and do what is best for you.

ANOTHER point that helps in the process is mindfulness and stress management. Incorporate mindfulness techniques, such as meditation and deep breathing to manage stress and anxiety. As already mentioned, hurdles are likely to occur in life, but it is not productive to be stressed about it. If you get too stressed, you will end up losing your motivation. Do not obsess too much about what will happen next. Being present in the moment can help you focus on your long-term goals instead of getting overwhelmed by setbacks.

The **EIGHTH** factor is visualization. As mentioned in a few chapters earlier, visualization is an important aspect for success. When you visualize your success and the journey to achieve it, you have already reached half of the destination. Create a picture of yourself in your mind where you are overcoming countless obstacles and reaching your goals. This can increase your motivation and belief in your ability to bounce back.

The **NEXT** important factor is to keep a journal. Keeping a journal becomes helpful in the long run. When you can maintain a journal to track your progress, setbacks, and emotions, it becomes easier to figure out the areas that need special attention. Note down what went wrong and how you can fix it. Reflect on your experiences and use your journal to remind yourself of your accomplishments and the progress that you have made so far.

ANOTHER point to keep in mind is to take breaks and practice self-care. Never glorify overworking or feeling burnt out. It does not help anyone in the end. All it does is— it drains you emotionally and physically. Taking breaks and practicing self-care is essential for both mental and physical health. Burnout can be a result of pushing too hard without giving yourself time to recharge. Engage in little activities that you enjoy and prioritize your well-being. Do things that make you happy. Go for a walk, a trip, bake a cake, write a poem. etc.

The **ELEVENTH** factor is to focus on the process, not just the outcome. While having a clear goal is essential, please focus on the process of working towards it. Trust the process. Always trust your intuition and know everything is happening for a reason. Focus on the journey, not the destination. Everything may not work out according to your choice, but in the end, the universe will always carve out what is best for you. Enjoy the journey and the small victories along the way rather than fixating solely on the result.

And **FINALLY**, have persistence and patience. Consistency is always the key to achieving what you desire. You have to be patient throughout the journey without expecting that you are just a step away from your destination. You have to understand that achieving your dreams takes time and persistence. Success achieved overnight is rare and often short-term. It takes years and years of hard work to reach your desired goal. Stay committed and patient, even when faced with setbacks that might temporarily slow your progress.

Always remember that when you start living the life of your dreams, there will always be hurdles along the way. But with honest intentions, hard work, and patience, there is no limit to what you can achieve. It is mandatory to keep in mind that setbacks are not indicators of your worth or potential. They are merely challenges that can be overcome with the right mindset, strategies, and support. By integrating these strategies into your approach, you can bounce back from setbacks and continue chasing your dreams with resilience and determination.

Somewhere, if you still feel overwhelmed by the fear of falling, remember the words of the journalist, author, and publisher of Forbes magazine, Rich Karlgaard— *"Early bloomers enjoy many advantages in affluent societies. But one huge disadvantage they face is that by dint of their youth and accomplishments, they give themselves credit for their success, more than the rest of us do. That's understandable: adolescents and young adults tend to be self-centered… The problem arises when early bloomers have a setback: either they put all the blame on themselves and fall into self-condemnation and paralysis, or they blame everyone else. Late bloomers tend to be more circumspect: they are able to see their own role in the adversity they face, without succumbing to self-condemnation or blame shifting."*

9

BE KIND TO STRANGERS

"Three things in human life are important. The first is to be kind. The second is to be kind. And the third is to be kind."

–Henry James

Whenever I stumble upon the word 'kindness' while reading anything, my brain automatically fades into a quote from the play *A Streetcar Named Desire* by Tennessee Williams— *"I have always depended on the kindness of strangers."* Regarding this particular quote, I have read an anonymous commentary that said — *"I have sometimes been sad that Tennessee Williams wrote that line for Blanche DuBois* (a character in the play)*, 'I have always depended on the kindness of strangers.' Many of us have been saved many times by the kindness of strangers, but after a while it sounds trite, like a bumper sticker. And that's what makes me sad, that a beautiful and true* *line comes to be used so often that it takes on the superficial sound of a bumper sticker."*

I have a firm belief that there are no strangers in life but only friends who you are yet to meet. Moreover, as a motorcyclist, I ultimately buy into the statement because, more often than not, it is the people whom you have never met who come to your aid when you are in need. Whether it is a punctured tire, a mechanical issue, a fuel shortage, or even a fall, it is always a stranger(s) who appears out of nowhere and offers help. Sometimes, despite having state-of-the-art GPS systems and fancy mobiles, we are saved by human networks while in the remotest parts of the world. Ask any rider about this, and they will tell you about the first responders whose faces they have never seen before the accident.

Many of us are alive today for the generosity and kindness of absolute strangers who pulled us out of ditches and rushed us to the nearby hospitals. I am sure this is true in every part of the world. Having done the bulk of my motorcycling in India, I can clearly vouch for the fact that the further away you go from home, whether it is the mountains of the north, remote villages of the east, or the tea gardens of the south, the human kindness shines through. People are always willing to help if you are in a difficult position, and they do this without expecting a reward or benefit. In a materialistic and selfish world, it is sometimes unbelievable that such behaviors exist today. But unless you experience it yourself, it may sound like an urban myth.

In July 2023, the Mountain State of Himachal Pradesh in India was hit by the worst deluge in living memory. As it was the peak tourist season, tens of thousands of tourists were visiting the state then. One of the most famous circuits in Himachal is the Spiti circuit, which is most popular with adventure-seeking motorcyclists and cyclists. The path from Kaza to Manali is considered to be the most treacherous part of this circuit, with unpaved boulder-ridden roads, high mountain passes, and multiple water crossings. When the deluge hit, the entire circuit got cut off from the rest of the state with heavy snowfall, making it impossible for the army rescue teams to reach. Over a thousand adventure seekers were stuck on the road without food or water. Subzero temperatures soon became life-threatening for some who were adequately protected.

In the Batal Valley, there was a small dhaba (shack), which was run by an elderly couple. It is popularly known as *"Chacha Chachi Dhaba"* and has been a favorite stop for most tourists who pass through the road. During the deluge, this little Dhaba became a significant rescue and rehab center where hundreds of stranded motorcyclists and cyclists were provided food and warm shelter by this elderly couple. They kept taking in every person who managed to reach their little dhaba and provided for everyone. They worked non-stop to keep people protected from the harsh elements outside, and that too for almost nothing. If you had the money, they took just the payment for the parathas, which were supplied hot, and if you didn't, then it was 'on the house.' All this while they were in touch with the army team, who had provided them with a wireless set for emergencies. The selfless act of this elderly couple saved many lives during that time of crisis. And this is nothing new. They have been doing it for forty years. *Chacha Chachi* dhaba is a point where stranded travelers and bikers take refuge when the weather turns hostile in that part of the world. And most of the people who get stranded and find refuge in *Chacha Chachi Dhaba* have never met the couple before and vice versa. The little institution of Chacha and Chachi is a shining beacon of selfless kindness to strangers that illuminates this wonderful planet of ours.

Having said that, kindness to strangers, though it's a selfless act, can be viewed from a more selfish perspective if I may say it, because kindness works. The world has been through a lot of things, but one thing that has remained constant throughout the passage of time was resilience and kindness. Being polite, humble, compassionate, and empathetic towards the people around you are really important and a few of the best ways to remain kind. Plato says, *"Be kind, for everyone you meet is fighting a harder battle."* Kindness is great for your brain, and there are enough social and cultural reasons behind that which perhaps you are already aware of. It is indeed one of the first values that parents try to build in their children. Yet as we grow up, we find our ability and scope of kindness decreasing day by day. In our fast-paced day and age, kindness is most often limited to people we know– our parents, kids, spouse, friends, co-workers, and not strangers. As individuals, we must try to integrate kindness into ourselves. You never know how a tiny act of kindness can bring about a change in someone's life. As we try to navigate our way through the various challenges life throws at us, we tend to grow more self-centered and caught up in our more problems to care about others, much less strangers. Therefore, the kindness we share with the world, too, becomes measured, driven by specific reasons, and, in many cases, self-serving.

The author Neil Gaiman says, *"I hope you will have a wonderful year, that you'll dream dangerously and outrageously, that you'll make something that didn't exist before you made it, that you will be loved and that you will be liked, and that you will have people to love and to like in return. And, most importantly (because I think there should be more kindness and more wisdom in the world right now), that you will, when you need to be, be wise, and that you will always be kind."* Kindness is like a muscle. The more you work at it, the stronger it becomes. In a world filled with unending struggle and pain, kindness is like a breath of fresh air that rejuvenates us with its purity and goodness and gives us the strength to persevere despite the hurdles. Like any other exercise, when you switch up the tactic you use, the results can be even more potent. One of the easiest ways to define kindness is— Kindness is the sincere and voluntary use of one's time, talent, and resources to better the lives of others, one's own life, and the world through genuine acts of love, compassion, generosity, and service. Therefore, if you are already in the habit of showing kindness to friends and family, find ways to be friendly, generous, and considerate to strangers too. Kindness is one of those unique gifts that only bears fruit when shared. In fact, multiple studies show that the person doing the act of kindness often benefits much more in terms of brain development than the one receiving the material reward of the act.

Here are a few benefits of being kind:

Firstly, kindness gives us what in common parlance is called a 'helper's high.' It is a surge of happy hormones in our brain. It refers to that euphoric feeling you get after helping an individual. Dopamine, Serotonin, and endogenous opioids are released when you engage in kind behavior, all of which has a significant contribution in helping you feel calm, reducing pain, and strengthening your executive functions and motivation. People who are kind know that life is difficult and often messy, and even then, they empathize with people and understand that they are giving their best to survive in this cruel world. In fact, kindness begins with understanding the fact that we all struggle.

Secondly, kind behavior also releases Oxytocin, which helps establish and strengthen the bond between the people engaged in the said behavior (the giver and the receiver), thereby reinforcing the community-building instinct. In fact, oxytocin is often called the love hormone as it plays a role in creating trust and building genuine bonds. Your brain releases oxytocin and serotonin when you help people. Serotonin even helps in regulating one's mood by producing a calming effect. After all, helping others is beneficial both for your physical and mental health. However, kindness is not equivalent to weakness. It is moving from 'I' to 'we,' seeing the bigger picture, and extending your strength and support to someone. In the book *The Light in the Heart*, Roy T. Bennett says, *"Be the reason someone smiles. Be the reason someone feels loved and believes in the goodness in people."* I strongly believe that when you can be the reason why someone does not lose hope in humanity, it is one of the greatest achievements in life.

Lastly, kindness reduces stress and anxiety. Some of you might have heard that doing good for someone is actually good for you. When we show up for people with kindness and compassion, the benefits go both ways. In fact, engaging in kind behavior while in a stressful frame of mind can dramatically reduce those negative feelings by stemming the surge of cortisol and other stress-response chemicals in your brain. The power of a kind gesture, a kind hand, a kind word, and a listening ear can have a huge impact on someone. When you see that you are the reason why someone felt happy, warm, and wanted, it will automatically make you happy. Therefore, try to follow the words of the Dalai Lama, *"My religion is very simple. My religion is kindness."*

So, why do we need to practice kindness?

Being kind and compassionate is a work of art. Not everyone is capable of doing it. Or I must say, everyone is capable of it, but they choose not to be kind. Much like every other thing we do with our brain, kindness also grows in practice. To a lot of people, showing kindness indicates going out of their way to do something humongous and unbelievable for others. But honestly, even tiny acts of kindness matters, just how Desmond Tutu iterates, *"Do your little bit of good where you are; it's those little bits of good put together that overwhelm the world."* The first step to being kind always begins with yourself. Therefore, be nice to yourself first. After that, spread kindness wherever you can. The more we share kindness, the more capacity for kindness we create in our brain.

Here's why we should make kindness a habit and not just one limited to our close circle of friends:

FIRSTLY, the science of neuroplasticity teaches us that repeating a particular behavior routinely changes the structure of your brain in the long run. Each small act of kindness we mindfully practice makes us a little more capable of being automatically kind in future. When you do something nice for others, your brain automatically feels good. When you keep repeating this behavior, your brain will keep you happier. However, do not do anything for the sake of expecting something in return. Be genuine and honest about your actions. In the end, life becomes far more pleasant when we see the goodness in others.

SECONDLY, kindness creates a ripple effect which is beneficial to a much larger scale than we can even conceive. Several studies have shown that receiving kindness, or even witnessing kind behavior in other people can benefit humans, and in turn creates a desire for repeating the same behavior. Your one small act of kindness today can actually inspire a great many people to behave kindly. This ripple effect of kind behavior strengthens the community as a whole and brings a lot of people closer in a positive way. Once you master the art of being kind without having expectations in return or having an ulterior motive, your life will overflow with an abundance of happiness. After all, as Mark Twain says, *"Kindness is a language that the deaf can hear, and the blind can see."*

When you do something kind for someone expecting something in return, that is essentially transactional behavior. It gives you a 'high' alright, but that is quite little compared to the surge of positivity your brain receives when your actions are completely altruistic, and that high is a lot more beneficial for your body and brain. Kindness will heal your soul from within. It will increase your self-esteem and remove all mental blocks. Therefore, let us pause a little today and take a good look at our surroundings. Everybody needs a little help to get by, why not be that one to provide that help? They will thank you, and so will your brain! Moreover, every tiny act of kindness you show today will have its way of returning to you. What goes around, always comes back around. Take a moment to pause and reflect on this quote that goes beyond our expressions and acts of kindness. This is from one of my favorite writers & poet— *"I've learned that people will forget what you said, people will forget what you did, but people will never forget how you made them feel"* – Maya Angelou. Here's another one from a comedian who added so much color to the black and white era, with just his comic timing— *"We think too much and feel too little. More than machinery, we need Humanity. More than cleverness, we need Kindness and Gentleness"* – Charlie Chaplin

10
MAKE YOUR OWN RULES

"It's your game: make up your own rules."
–Anonymous

Since you have invested so much of your time to read so far, it clearly indicates you want to make a change in your life. Well, I have the most crucial piece of advice or recommendation for you— ignore everything that you have read so far. I do not want you to blindly follow the masses or believe in what someone else has faith in. I know that sounds quite counterintuitive and may be confusing. However, I sincerely want to make an appeal to you to only pay heed to any recommendation or suggestion made before in this book if it makes sense to you because everyone's reality is different.

What can work out for one person may not work out for someone else. I want you to have your own experiences and form your own beliefs. Having said that, I have compiled this book based on my personal experiences and after having spoken to many people who have made a big difference in their lives without having everything working in their favor. These people took charge of their lives and made something happen rather than blame outside forces for their life challenges. My in-depth conversation and interviews with them have given me a few recipes, which I have shared with you beyond my personal experience, but then pick it or adapt it only, and only if it makes sense to your life right now. The author Robert A. Heinlein perfectly summarizes this in his quote, *"I am free, no matter what rules surround me. If I find them tolerable, I tolerate them; if I find them too obnoxious, I break them. I am free because I know that I alone am morally responsible for everything I do."* Therefore, I urge you to create your own rules.

Now, what do I mean by creating your own rules?

I want you to come up with a set of principles which you believe you can fully live by, and it can help you change the status quo and drive you towards your dream fulfilment. In fact, I want you to live by the words of the Dalai Lama— *"Know the rules well, so you can break them effectively."* The previous chapters could be just inspirational pointers towards those principles, but you should choose the ones that make sense to you and probably write a few that are missing and something that you can intentionally add to your life. After all, when you have your own rules, it serves as a reminder of what you are good at and can live by. Personal rules act as a sturdy lighthouse in most cases. Despite the weather outside, the lighthouse performs and functions every day. It is exactly the reason why we need rules that we can live by.

The idea is to make a change or live a life we are incredibly proud of. Falling or failing is neither the end nor the deterrent that should keep us from who we truly can become. Thus, my sincere attempt was to share with you a series of thoughts and ideas which I believe can inspire you to do new things. As human beings, we are incredibly blessed by the tremendous power to drive our life to the destiny that we truly deserve. Many of us do not understand that our decisions shape our destiny or that the lack of decisions we make also impacts our destiny. Therefore, if you can align yourself with the principles I shared so far, and if they inspire you to take action and not be deterred by setbacks, give yourself a chance to do something different. Something that will make you inherently very proud. If this book motivates you to do new things or take the road less traveled by, I have added something back to this universe, which has given me a lot.

As humans, we are individuals of our own. As individuals, we are less likely to follow someone else's rules and more likely to follow our own. Similarly, as a rider, I have formed my own riding style rather than adopting or copying someone else's style. I ride in a way that makes me feel safe yet enjoy the thrill of riding a motorcycle. It may be too aggressive for some or maybe too defensive for others. But my style has provided me with what I seek from the passion called motorcycle touring. The world that we live in is organized around rules. In school and college, we learn "rules" to excel in life. But as a grown-up, you are free to make your own rules and create your destiny. I believe the words of the author, Mandy Hale, perfectly align with what you have read so far— *"You'll learn, as you get older, that rules are made to be broken. Be bold enough to live life on your terms, and never, ever apologize for it. Go against the grain, refuse to conform, take the road less traveled instead of the well-beaten path. Laugh in the face of adversity, and leap before you look. Dance as though EVERYBODY is watching. March to the beat of your own drummer. And stubbornly refuse to fit in."*

Now, what are the advantages to setting your own rules?

First, you can work on your own strengths. Well, no one knows you better than you. You are aware of your strengths and shortcomings. Once you know what the areas you are lagging behind in, you can work on them efficiently. Your strength might be simplifying a complex process or motivating another person. Only you will know the truth. I want you to find your own strengths. Polish on your strength areas every day. Be the best in whatever you do. I want you to be a better version of yourself every day. I want you to understand who you are, what you want from life and go ahead to fulfil your purpose. In short, I want you to learn to fish rather than be gifted a fish.

Second, you know your own limitations. A part of knowing your strength signifies you know your limitations too. Every human has their own weakness. Admitting them and acknowledging your limitations makes you strong. Only you know how much time you have. Only you are aware of your physical and emotional limits. Knowing what you are not good at is more important than knowing what you are actually good at. Figuring out your weakness and turning it into your strength is an ultimate game changer. However, if you cannot convert your weakness into your strength, at least develop a positive mindset to overcome any situation. You can build the future of your dreams when you leverage your strengths and avoid your weaknesses. However, that decision lies only in your hands.

Third, you will become more disciplined. Once you create your own rules to win in life, you will have to be more disciplined. You will have to make sure you are dedicated enough to attain the accomplishments you choose to have. You will be committed enough to work on your core areas and journal your journey. You will never learn to start something new if you do not have self-discipline. Everything always starts with you. When you create your own goals and work hard to reach them, something happens. You feel a sense of accomplishment. Make sure you do not get disheartened if you find a few hurdles on the way. You begin to tear down the self-defeating beliefs that you have held onto for so long. You metamorphose into a new person altogether.

Finally, your own rules lead to longer-lasting change. Once you start setting and reaching your own goals, it becomes a habit. Once you start implementing those changes daily, it fills your subconscious to keep doing it daily. It is that deeply-ingrained habit which will lead to long lasting change. Once you follow your own rules, you grow into a better human altogether. Whatever you do today will impact your tomorrow. Therefore, the power lies in your hands. Following someone else's rules does not hold the same power. Create your own rules and be responsible for your choices. Your own rules allow you to choose your own rigor and pace. Sometimes, slow changes are the best changes for you.

The path to a meaningful, impactful life often means forging a trail that no one has ventured on before. The dreamers, innovators, and change-makers of the world are those who dared to write their own rules. You, too, can be one of them. We cannot be liberated and play the game of life without abiding by the rules, but the rules have to be adapted constantly in line with our experiences. From the moment we are born, societal norms and expectations begin to shape our perceptions and decisions. We are told what to do and what to refrain from doing. We are told to put everyone else first before ourselves. But that need not always be the case.

You can choose yourself before others. It is not selfishness. We are taught to walk down predefined paths, often stemming from centuries-old beliefs and values. But here is a thought—the path that worked for one might not work for all. Hence, we should abide by the words of Pablo Picasso *"Learn the rules like a pro, so you can break them like an artist."* Steve Jobs, Co-founder of Apple Inc., once said, *"Don't let the noise of others' opinions drown out your own inner voice."* Steve Jobs knew that to innovate and revolutionize technology, he could not stick to the existing playbook; he had to write his own. There are countless people who have written their own rules and succeeded: Frida Kahlo, MS Dhoni, Deigo Maradona, A R Rahman, Shah Rukh Khan, Warren Buffet, Oprah Winfrey, Elon Musk, and the list of people who did not play the game as per others' rules is a large one. They did not give in to the opinions of others. They built their own kingdom. The key point is that they knew what could work the best for them.

So, how can you craft your own rule book?

The very **FIRST** thing is to identify your core values. You have to build your rules according to your principles. Your rules should resonate with your inner beliefs. You should ask yourself— what matters the most to me? Integrity? Creativity? Compassion? Take a deep breath and figure out your answers. Your values are the compass guiding your journey. You have to stick to your beliefs and keep working on your goals every day.

The **SECOND** step is to question the status quo: You have to understand that making your own rules means breaking away from societal norms. Just because "it's always been done this way" does not mean it is always the best way. You must have the courage to stand up for yourself and not 'fit in' to please society. In the end, nobody will be there for you, so you have every right to choose what is best for you. Like Elon Musk's approach to transportation with Tesla and SpaceX, you must challenge existing paradigms and dare to think differently.

The **THIRD** step is to surround yourself with enablers: Be it mentors, friends, or books, ensure you have a solid support system. As mentioned earlier, having a solid support system, or having people with positive energy around works as a boon for your journey. When Oprah Winfrey started her talk show, several people doubted her approach. But she had a team that believed in her vision, and together they transformed daytime television. Therefore, you need to have people around you who will always uplift you and set the right kind of morale.

Finally, the **LAST** step is to iterate and evolve: You must always remember that your rulebook is not cast in stone. With every year passing by, there will be new creative things to look at and learn from. As you grow, and as the world changes, your rules should adapt. Have an open mindset. Do not be stuck with the same rules forever. As time flies, understand what works better for you in the current generation which you will be living in. Create new rules and learn better. Remember, it is a guide and not a straitjacket.

Your life is a blank canvas, and you are its painter. You have the liberty of splashing it with the most extravagant, beautiful, and spectacular colors by doing what you love and desire. You can choose to reproduce existing masterpieces, or you can dip your brush into your soul and paint your own magnum opus. Writing your own rules is not about rebelling for the sake of rebellion. It is about understanding that the symphony of your life should be composed of notes that resonate with your unique spirit. So, what are you waiting for? Pick up that pen, that brush, that instrument. Start writing, painting, and creating new things. The world is waiting for the rules you will write and the dreams you will chase. Embrace the journey and live a life truly worth living.

On days when you feel lost or fail to understand how to create your own rules, I want you to remember these words – *"There is no list of rules. There is one rule. The rule is: there are no rules. Happiness comes from living as you need to, as you want to. As your inner voice tells you to. Happiness comes from being who you actually are instead of who you think you are supposed to be. Being traditional is not traditional anymore. It's funny that we still think of it that way. Normalize your lives, people. You don't want a baby? Don't have one. I don't want to get married? I won't. You want to live alone? Enjoy it. You want to love someone? Love someone. Don't apologize. Don't explain. Don't ever feel less than. When you feel the need to apologize or explain who you are, it means the voice in your head is telling you the wrong story. Wipe the slate clean. And rewrite it. No fairy tales. Be your own narrator. And go for a happy ending. One foot in front of the other. You will make it."*

CONCLUSION

To summarize everything that we contemplated so far— life opens up in amazing ways when we are ready to let it flow. You may not want to make some tectonic shifts in life, but doing something new is the gift that keeps giving, no matter how small it might be. Life has this amazing ability to give you a richer experience and, hence, a richer life. All you have to do is to say yes when that opportunity presents itself. Deep down in your gut, you will know what is good for you and what is not. In order to develop that capability and perception, you should be mentally open to change long before the opportunity arrives. You just cannot wait till the opportunity comes to figure out things. So, if not anything else, just be open to opportunities and have richer experiences.

Let the magic take over from there all. My countless motorcycle journeys have given me much richer life experiences than all the work achievements from my corporate life have ever given me. Mind you, I am not putting down what the corporate world has given me. I am extremely grateful for the countless achievements, successes, and relationships that I have built over the years. However, the motorcycle journeys and the explorations have given me gifts that are long-lasting and life-altering in many ways. I have made more friends and much deeper relationships. I have reached some of the most beautiful parts of the world that I never thought I would reach. I met people who I had never thought would meet and I have been able to make a difference to a very large number of underprivileged children. Their lives have changed through the charity which I managed to support through my motorcycling endeavors and my organization along with two partners. These two partners, who are like my brothers, are always willing to try something new. I would not have had this opportunity if they were unwilling to jump at the deep end.

Come to think of it, this book would not have existed if not for my passion for riding. It has changed my life and gave me the experiences that I believe will be valuable to you. Hence, this book is also a result of taking the road less travelled by many. It was not easy for me to do every new thing that I had done, especially after spending close to twenty-seven years in one industry and reaching the top levels, then to change to something completely different. Nevertheless, things became easier when I started doing it. It was challenging initially but got easier when I started learning. Therefore, through this book, what I hope to share with you is probably a small set of guardrails or guiding posts rather than rules that might help you, and I hope it will inspire you to start saying yes to life's opportunities.

If we recap what we have majorly imbibed through this book is— embracing the unknown. It is about facing the unknown and saying "yes" and that alone will not do unless we are a bit prepared for the journey. We should be willing to take some calculated risk, and trusting your instinct is not about being risky. We have also learned about focusing on and enjoying the journey rather than just about getting to the destination. Focusing on the opportunities and the road is far more beneficial. Of course, the temptation of shortcuts lowers, but we are out to get a richer experience. So, experience is greater than the outcome for us. Therefore, we have learned to avoid shortcuts. The reality of falsehood does happen. What we do after the fall is all that matters. It is not that anyone who has ever done anything great has never tasted defeat. But what they did after that made all the difference. Moreover, the universe acts through absolutely unknown strangers in terms of helping us reach our destination. Hence, let us be kind to the world around us and also to strangers. Some of them might be the angels that the universe is sending to help us reach where we are reaching. Finally, if you believe these nine rules or guiding posts do not work for you, write your own rules. More often than not, when you create your own rules, you are more or less creating your destiny, and you are more likely to follow those things.

While I was at L&K Saatchi & Saatchi, there was a very inspiring ethos that governed the culture of the organization. At Saatchi, we believed that 'Nothing is impossible' and it formed the foundation on which we built our values, personality and even our solutions. I found the ethos deeply inspirational at a personal level too. I started witnessing some amazing results both in my professional life and personal life when I removed the limiting beliefs and self-doubts. Nothing is impossible if you truly believe in yourself, back your conviction and put in the honest effort. Therefore, don't just write your own rules but live by them too.

My humble plea to you, dear reader, is to let go of the tight grip on the handlebar of life and let life guide you to the most rewarding journey in all walks of life. The death grip, as we motorcyclists call it, which is about holding on to the handle for dear life, is a surefire reason for most crashes. You have to hold the handle only to provide the guiding function, not as a crutch. If you hold on to what you have so dearly, it may take you to places you don't want to go or will not take you to beautiful places which you could have gone to. Therefore, you must learn to let go.

It is okay to fall; you will get up and get on with it, richer by experience and resolve. That is how we go further in life. Some of the 10 signposts I shared are what can bolster one in the event of a fall. Or they may be a great 'pick me up emotion' once we dust ourselves and step forward after the fall. I believe my effort of writing this book is something similar. As a first-time author, I am willing to fall and learn from it. If at least one person who reads the book could turn his life around and pursue what he has dreamed about all his life, then I think the effort of writing this book was worth it. I pray that thousands of people out there get inspired by this book. If you are one of the thousand, I will be the happiest, and I shall consider my little endeavor a grand success.

So, what are you waiting for? Go on and boldly step forward towards the life that you deserve, without the fear of failing, because now you have the license for it.

All the best for your journey!

ABOUT THE AUTHOR

Before starting his second innings as an entrepreneur, Anil had been a storyteller on behalf of brands for most of his career. He spent 27 years in the marketing & advertising industry at the helm of globally renowned company like Saatchi & Saatchi in India. He was the Co-founder of one of the biggest independent agencies in India - Law & Kenneth, which was merged with Saatchi & Saatchi in 2014, which Anil went on to lead for years. He played a significant role in helping many MNC brands script their success in India. But his core expertise lies in building powerful local brands from scratch & helping them stand on their own amongst global giants. He has worked on blue chip brands like Coca-Cola, Dettol, Renault, Sony, HSBC, Emirates, Skoda, Thomas Cook, Hero Motocorp, ITC, Pepperfry, Jockey & Kent, etc.

Anil has been ranked 15th most influential person in the advertising and media industry in India by Economic Times, India's leading business daily, in the last decade. Anil is currently in his second innings as an entrepreneur, board advisor, and investor. Apart from Goodwind Moto Tours, he co-founded The Pretty Geeky, a children's edu-games company, an investor in an OTT content creation company and a specialty Ecom portal in the luxury space.

He is an independent director on the board of one of the largest jewelry companies in India - Kalyan Jewellers. He is on the board of a global packaging solutions company – Pacfora. Apart from this, Anil is also a partner and Executive Director of a top-rated business consultancy - Equitor Value Advisory. Anil is also an enthusiastic and experimentative cook, a passionate fan of Arsenal FC, a compulsive traveler, and a self-appointed master of red wine.

www.ingramcontent.com/pod-product-compliance
Lightning Source LLC
Chambersburg PA
CBHW032358040426
42451CB00006B/51